THE STATUE OF
OUR SOULS

Revival in Islamic Thought and Activism

M. Fethullah Gülen

Light

New Jersey
2005

Published by The Light, Inc.
26 Worlds Fair Dr. Suite C
Somerset, New Jersey, 08873, USA

www.thelightpublishing.com
http://en.fgulen.com

Translated from Turkish by Muhammed Çetin

Library of Congress Cataloging-in-Publication Data

Gulen, Fethullah.
  [Ruhumuzun heykelini dikerken. English]
  The statue of our souls : revival in Islamic thought and activism /
Fethullah Gulen ; translated from Turkish by Muhammed Çetin.-- 1st English ed.
    p. cm.
  Includes index.
  ISBN 1-932099-87-5
  1. Islamic renewal. I. Title.
BP60.G8513 2005
297'.09'0511--dc22

                              2005007472

Printed by
Çağlayan A.Ş., Izmir - Turkey
July 2005

Cover design: İhsan Demirhan
Cover photograph: Selimiye Mosque, Edirne

THE STATUE OF
OUR SOULS

Revival in Islamic Thought and Activism

TABLE OF CONTENTS

ABOUT THE AUTHOR

B orn in Erzurum, in eastern Turkey, in 1941, M. Fethullah Gülen is an Islamic scholar and thinker, and a prolific writer and poet. He was trained in the religious sciences by several celebrated Muslim scholars and spiritual masters. Gülen also studied the principles and theories of modern social and physical sciences. Based on his exceptional skills in learning and focused self-study, he soon surpassed his peers. In 1959, after attaining excellent examination results, he was awarded a state preacher's license (in Edirne), and was promoted to a post in Izmir, Turkey's third largest province, in 1966. It was here that Gülen started to crystallize his theme and expand his audience base. In his sermons and speeches he emphasized the pressing social issues of the times: his particular aim was to urge the younger generation to harmonize intellectual enlightenment with wise spirituality and a caring, humane activism.

Gülen did not restrict himself to teaching in the inner cities. He traveled around the provinces in Anatolia and lectured not only in mosques, but also at town meetings and corner coffee houses. This enabled him to reach a more representative cross-section of the population and to attract the attention of the academic community, especially the student body. The subject matter of his speeches, whether formal or informal, was not restricted explicitly to religious questions; he also talked about education, science, Darwinism, about the economy and social justice. It was the depth and quality of his speeches on such a wide range of topics that most impressed the academic community, and won their attention and respect.

Gülen retired from formal teaching duties in 1981, having inspired a whole generation of young students. His efforts, dating from the 1960s, especially in educational reform, have made him one of the best-known and respected figures in Turkey. From 1988 to 1991, he gave a series of sermons as preacher emeritus in some of the most famous mosques in major population centers, while continuing to deliver his message in the form of popular conferences, not only in Turkey, but also in Western Europe.

MAIN IDEAS

In his speeches and writings Gülen envisions a twenty-first century in which we shall witness the birth of a spiritual dynamic that will revitalize long-dormant moral values; an age of tolerance, understanding, and international cooperation that will ultimately lead, through intercultural dialogue and a sharing of values, to a single, inclusive civilization. In the field of education, he has spearheaded the establishment of many charitable organizations to work for the welfare of the community, both within and without Turkey. He has inspired the use of mass media, notably television, to inform the public, of matters of pressing concern to them, individually and collectively.

Gülen believes the road to justice for all is dependent on the provision of an adequate and appropriate universal education. Only then will there be sufficient understanding and tolerance to secure respect for the rights of others. To this end, he has, over the years, encouraged the social elite and community leaders, powerful industrialists as well as small businessmen, to support quality education. With donations from these sources, educational trusts have been able to establish many schools, both in Turkey and abroad.

Gülen has stated that in the modern world the only way to get others to accept your ideas is by persuasion. He describes those who resort to force as being intellectually bankrupt; people will always demand freedom of choice in the way they run their affairs and in their expression of their spiritual and religious values. Democracy, Gülen argues, in spite of its many shortcomings, is now the only viable political system, and people should strive to modernize and consolidate democratic institutions in order to build a society where individual rights and freedoms are respected and protected, where equal opportunity for all is more than a dream.

INTERFAITH AND INTERCULTURAL ACTIVITIES

Since his retirement, Gülen has concentrated his efforts on establishing a dialogue among the factions representing different ideologies, cultures, religions and nations. In 1999, his paper "The Necessity of Interfaith Dialogue" was presented to the Parliament of World's Religions in Cape Town, December 1-8. He maintains that "dialogue is a must" and that people, regardless of nation or political borders, have far more in common than they realize.

Given all of this, Gülen considers it both worthwhile and necessary for a sincere dialogue to be established in order to increase mutual understanding. To this end, he has helped to establish the Journalists and Writers Foundation (1994), whose activities to promote dialogue and tolerance among all strata of the society have been warmly welcomed by people from almost all walks of life. Again to this end, Gülen visits and receives leading figures, not only from among the Turkish population, but from all over the world. Pope John Paul II at the Vatican, the late John O'Connor, Archbishop of New York, Leon Levy, former president of The Anti-Defamation League are among many leading representatives of world religions with whom Gülen has met to discuss dialogue and take initiatives in this respect. In Turkey, the Vatican's Ambassador to Turkey, the Patriarch of the Turkish Orthodox Church, the Patriarch of the Turkish Armenian community, the Chief Rabbi of the Turkish Jewish community and many other leading figures in Turkey have frequently met with him, portraying an example of how sincere dialogue can be established between people of faith.

In his meeting with Pope John Paul II at the Vatican (1998), Gülen presented a proposal to take firm steps to stop the conflict in the Middle East via collaborative work on this soil, a place where all three religions originated. In his proposal, he also underlined the fact that science and religion are in fact two different aspects that emanate from the same truth: "Humankind from time to time has denied religion in the name of science and denied science in the name of religion, arguing that the two present conflicting views. All knowledge belongs to God and religion is from God. How then can the two be in conflict? To this end, our joint efforts directed at inter-religious dialogue can do much to improve understanding and tolerance among people."

Gülen released a press declaration renouncing the September 11th terrorist attacks on the USA, which he regarded as a great blow to world peace that unfairly tarnished the credit of believers: ". . . terror can never be used in the name of Islam or for the sake of any Islamic ends. A terrorist cannot be a Muslim and a Muslim cannot be a terrorist. A Muslim can only be the representative and symbol of peace, welfare, and prosperity."

Gülen's efforts for worldwide peace have been echoed at conferences and symposiums. "The Peaceful Heroes Symposium" (April 11-13, 2003) at the University of Texas, Austin, produced a list of peacemakers over 5,000 years of human history. Gülen was mentioned among contemporary heroes of peace, in a list which includes names such as Jesus, Buddha, Mohandas Gandhi, Martin Luther King, Jr., and Mother Teresa.

In March 2004, the Spirituality Foundation of Kyrgyzstan awarded Gülen with its "Intersociety Adaptation and Contribution to Peace Prize" for his contribution to international peace through his thoughts and activities in education.

Gülen contributes to a number of journals and magazines. He writes the editorial page for several magazines. He writes the lead article for *The Fountain*, *Yeni Ümit*, *Sızıntı*, and *Yağmur*, leading popular and spiritual thought magazines in Turkey. He has written more than forty books, hundreds of articles, and recorded thousands of audio and videocassettes. He has delivered innumerable speeches on many social and religious issues. Some of his books—many of which have been best-sellers in Turkey—have been made available in English translations, such as, *The Messenger of God: Muhammad - An Analysis of the Prophet's Life*, *Questions and Answers about Faith*, *Pearls of Wisdom*, *Prophet Muhammad as Commander*, *The Essentials of the Islamic Faith*, *Towards the Lost Paradise*, *Key Concepts in the Practice of Sufism*. A number have also been translated into German, Russian, Albanian, Japanese, Indonesian, and Spanish.

The educational trusts inspired by Gülen have established countless non-profit voluntary organizations—foundations and associations—in Turkey and abroad which support many scholarships.

Though a well-known public figure, Gülen has always shied away from involvement in formal politics. Gülen's admirers include leading journalists, academics, TV personalities, politicians, and Turkish and foreign state authorities. They see in him a true innovator and unique social reformer who practices what he preaches. They see him as a peace activist, an intellectual, a religious scholar, a mentor, author and poet, a great thinker and spiritual guide who has devoted his life to seeking the solutions for society's ills and spiritual needs. They see the movement he helped to nurture as a movement dedicated to education, but an education of the heart and soul as well as of the mind, aimed at reviving and invigorating the whole being to achieve competence and providing goods and services useful to others.

PREFACE

Those who follow Gülen's world of ideas closely will see that what he wrote or preached 15-20 years ago and the ideas he puts forward today are in no way different nor do they conflict in essence; on the contrary, all of his works and speeches interpret one another and gradually lead toward a main idea. He has written a library full of works over the years, and all of these are focused on subjects like the tremors and collapses that the Muslim world, in particular, the Turkish nation, have gone through, the failure to represent Islam as it should be and the reasons for this, the realization of a revival in the Muslim world, the representation of Islam, once again, on a universal scale and the basic dynamics and characteristics of the generation that will carry out this duty. When viewed from this aspect, the works of Gülen voice the same message forming a great symphony when brought together. *The Statue of Our Souls* is a systematic and thorough expression of the ideas the author has suggested for a revival and the efforts made to realize the same. It is oriented to revival in thought and action and provides guidelines for—in his own words—"the inheritors of the Earth."

The book first presents us with an overall view of the condition of the Muslim world, and we see that where Muslims are to be found, there exists a paradoxical life. On the one hand, there is depression, weakness, the people are approaching the edge of the abyss through ignorance and superstition; yet, on the other hand, people in general are more inclined to turning to God and they struggle for revival almost everywhere . . . you

can see people who are thirsty for the peace and security promised by Islam. The depression, which the author terms "days of
decline," has been the continuously bleeding wound of the
Muslim world over the past few centuries.

Muslims, who once turned the world into "a dimension of
Paradise," sacrificed the religion, their real source of power, to
this world and they lost the perfect balance they had established
between the universe, humanity, and life. In this way, they
rejected the heritage of a thousand years, and tried to replace it
with new, but weak building blocks incompatible with the primordial nature of humanity. However, it is a reality that in spite
of all the traumas, depressions, and storms of the days of
decline, the idea of a revival has always waited in some remote
corner for the day when it will prevail.

For the sake of a revival, in other words for the sake of
repairing the shaken Muslim logic, of compensating for deviations, and of establishing a new and healthy life, the entire
Muslim world needs to go through a "resurrection." This revival
is one that will protect the origin of the religion within the
width and universality promised by the flexible principles of
Islam, a revival that will meet the needs of all classes of people
and embrace all aspects of life in every time and in every place.

It has been pointed out that humanity, life, and the universe
should be approached from an Islamic perspective, and that it is
an obligation of the Muslim societies that have pushed aside
Islamic logic, thought, and concepts to be encouraged toward a
renewal in all its depths.

Those who undertake this heavy responsibility and who
help to realize a universal change should be a new type of people. The author calls them "the inheritors of the Earth," and he
describes them as people who reflect the spirit of the Prophet
and Qur'anic morals.

In a way, *The Statue of Our Souls* describes and analyzes this
renaissance that has already begun. This renaissance is a process

that can be realized when an entire nation returns to its own spiritual roots. Our nation, which has lived a revival a few times over, can prevent illnesses like "passion, laziness, seeking fame, selfishness, worldliness, narrow-mindedness, the use of brute force" with exalted human values like "contentedness, courage, modesty, altruism, knowledge and virtue, and the ability to think universally"; it is then that we can say a Qur'an-oriented change back to our primordial nature will have been realized.

This resurrection, or great renaissance, is to be realized by the members of the nation who will share the same reviving spirit completely. In this way, our nation will take hold of its long-lost trust again, and aim to make the world a paradise-like place. *The Statue of Our Souls* both idealizes and voices a horizon of thought, as well as analyzing the sociological and historical obstacles that stand before the re-construction of the Muslim world. Gülen, however, never loses trust in the nation which bears the fire of a revival deep inside and he feels connected to them through an eternal hope.

It can be seen, in fact, that the central theme of this collection of Gülen's writings is an exhortation to a determined self-improvement in his followers and amongst Muslims generally. Muslims must strive to become worthy of the promise made to us. He alludes repeatedly to God's promise to the faithful:

> Before this We wrote in the Psalms, after the Message (Given to Moses): "My servants, the righteous, shall inherit the earth." (Anbiya 21:105)

Gülen echoes the great teacher Rumi in telling us not to ignore the doctrine of causes, not to sit around heedlessly waiting for God's favor, but rather to exert ourselves endlessly in order to transform this broken world into the world of peace and justice, in accordance with the Will of God. Again, like Rumi, he points out that it is in this, our willing submission to the Will of God that the only true freedom is found, that paradoxically it is this submission, and only this submission which can free us from slavery to meaningless and ultimately destructive whim, fancy, folly and temptation. He indicates the path to freedom and eternal life, sometimes by giving us quite simple and direct instructions which can be applied in the worldly contexts in which we find ourselves, sometimes by ornate descriptions of the spiritual delights to be found on the path and at the destination, and he urges us again and again that we should, of our own free will, follow that straight path.

Gülen's work is a constant exhortation to greater effort, greater knowledge, greater self-control and restraint. He reminds us that these are the qualities for which God will reward us. He reminds us of the value of patience and of how many times in the pages of the Qur'an we are urged to be patient and endure. He does not advocate and has never advocated the use of violence to attain political ends. "The days of getting things done by brute force are over," he tells us. "In today's enlightened world the only way to get others to accept your ideas is by persuasion and convincing argument. Those who use brute force to reach their goals are intellectually bankrupt." He is not an "externalist," one who thinks that Islam can be imposed on others from without by the forceful application of *shari'a*. He wants the renewal of society to start from within the heart. While acknowledging the importance of law and order in society, he does not believe that virtue can be instilled by force nor that the virtuous society is built by repression. Far from it, he protests wherever freedom is restricted unnecessarily. Gülen adheres to the Qur'anic injunction that the different tribes and nations which were all made by God should learn from each other and hence does not reject all the technical, political and cultural aspects of Western modernity, such as democracy, parliamentarianism, and scientific education. Rather he advises giving such institutions an Islamic dimension and in this way avoiding both the negative effects of a wholly secularist ideology and the stagnation and fossilization of a religious society which cannot adapt to its environment.

In Gülen's eyes and in his life Islam is not the fragile, fossilized museum relic which modern secularists would like it to be. For him and for the many who agree with him it is not only vital and alive but our only way, our true connection with the Real, with the True, with the Source of our life. As such the injunctions of God in the Qur'an and Sunna and in the cosmos must be re-examined, rebuilt, restored in every age in the light of advancing knowledge and changing states. His jihad is not the dark sinful despair and desperate struggle of extremism which sees itself as pitted against a too mighty enemy but effort along with the calm confidence of faith, the optimism of one who believes that God has placed in human hearts the desire for goodness and wholeness, endowed him with understanding, and the belief that the Muslim's task is to draw this out gently and bring it to bloom.

A major concept that occurs as a theme throughout the book is Gülen's understanding of "nation." Although this concept refers particularly to the Muslim world and the Turkish nation in the context of their roles in shaping human history, as major players and representatives of global peace, there is certainly more to it than just the concept of one particular nation, especially when we look with Gülen's vision and his idealism of dialogue and tolerance. In this book, Gülen addresses globally valid solutions for freedom and an honorable stand which any suppressed community could resort to. The motivating ethos behind Gülen's career as clearly manifested in numerous dialogue activities and education initiatives is one of a worldwide peace which will be accomplished by the participation of all nations. Gülen's definition of nation does not comprise one race; Anatolia has always been a land of diverse ethnic groups throughout history, which form one united nation today. Exempt from any chauvinist characteristic, he addresses to the colorful mosaic of Anatolia which is like a crucible for peoples that have come from Central Asia, Balkans, and Mesopotamia.

Finally, as one of the most significant thinkers and activists of Turkey, indeed of the modern Muslim world, Gülen has concerned himself throughout his life's work with finding and enacting solutions for the tremendous sense of strain, alienation, weakness, defeat, and disintegration felt in the Muslim world since the fall of the Ottoman State at the beginning of the twentieth century. Unlike many other Muslim leaders, however, he neither denies reality and turns his back on modernity, nor does he fall into bitterness, incomprehension and fury, but rather he exhorts Muslims to educate themselves, control themselves and use their own resources to regain and restore their culture, their identity and the observance of their religion. His is essentially a message of peace and hope, a message that is best conveyed in *The Statue of Our Souls*.

We would like to thank Hakan Yeşilova for supervising all the editorial process during the publication of this book; Korkut Altay for invaluable criticisms and especially for his collaboration in checking the translation against the original, and Jane Louise Kandur for copyediting and refining the manuscript in terms of consistency in style.

Ruth Woodhall
Muhammed Çetin

THE WORLD IN THE WOMB

In the recent past, the Islamic world as a whole has lived through its most depressed periods, whether considered from the point of view of faith, morality, modes of thought, education, industry, customs, traditions, or practices.

Yet once Muslims were far more distinguished in their piety; they were more devout, more correct and decent in their morality, more stable and wholesome in their customs and practices, more worthy to dominate world affairs on account of their social and political horizons and their more progressive and sophisticated modes of thought. They practiced their religion without fault or failure, perfected their morality, understood the place and value of science and knowledge, always managed to be ahead of the level of learning and the standards of the era in which they lived, and properly appreciated and balanced the relation and interaction between inspiration, reason, and experience.

That is why they were able to rule such vast lands, from the Pyrenees to the Indian Ocean, from Kazan to Somalia, from Poitiers to the Great Wall of China, with the best administrative and governing system known up to that time, and their ideals aroused the admiration of all. While other peoples were experiencing the darkest ages in their history, the Muslims, in the territories under their jurisdiction, enjoyed and extended to other peoples systems of governance that were idealized as a utopia or an earthly paradise.

What a pity that this part of the world deviated and distanced itself from the historical dynamics and Islamic values which had kept it standing upright through the ages, and that it became slave to ignorance, immorality, superstition, and carnal pleasure. This is when Islamic civilization began its slide into the abyss of darkness and great disappointments; when it began to be dragged into one crisis after another; when it became scattered everywhere, like the beads of a rosary when the string has been snapped; when it was left under the stairs, like pages fallen from a book with a loose binding; when it was profoundly shaken by fruitless rivalries, bent double under the weight of a thousand disputes, bewildered and stupefied into singing the songs of freedom even as it moaned and groaned bitterly under the most shameful, humiliating enslavement; when it began to lack a strong sense of identity, yet was very strong in its selfishness; when it took a stand in defiance of God and the Prophet arguing them to be taboos, yet was in the grip of so many others; when it began to become "the most wretched of all."

Despite many efforts of ill-meaning detractors, from within and without, the recent gloomy period has in fact not lasted long. Muslims today, who now account for about a fifth of the human population, are striving for a fresh revival, nearly everywhere in the Islamic world and are trying to save themselves from this accursed era of enslavement. Particularly in recent times, the fact that they have had to face new calamities every day has heightened the spiritual attentiveness of Muslims, has given momentum to their return to God, and has aroused and excited their resolve.

As we were certain of both the conformity between the spirit of Islam and the human nature, with its support for both the material and spiritual advancement of humans, and with its unique quality to balance this world and the hereafter, we survived with breathing, "the truth will always be victorious; the truth can never be defeated"[1]; and we day and night were in expectation to *"The (happy) end is for those who are righteous,"*[2] never losing hope. And today we are able to witness, in all walks of life, a fast-growing inclination to Islam; we now can observe that Islam is coming to the fore and gaining prominence in a vast area, from the United States to the Asian steppes, from Scandinavia to Australia.

Although many missionary activities of different faiths are systematically carried out by various groups, they have been unable to arouse one tenth of the interest and warmth in their respective religion that greets Islam. Today, throughout many continents of the world, thousands of people choose to embrace Islam every year, taking refuge in the light of the Qur'an, even though they know that they may be sentenced to some form of starvation and misery.

Unless we fail to keep our loyalty to God[3] and glad tidings of the divine message will be experienced once more:

> When there comes the help of God and the victory, And you see men entering the religion of God in companies, Then celebrate the praise of your Lord, and ask His forgiveness; surely He is oft returning (to mercy). (Nasr 110:1-3)

From America to Europe, from the Balkans to the Great Wall of China and the heart of Africa, indeed, almost everywhere, faith, hope, security, and therefore, peace and contentment will be experienced once more under the umbrella of Islam; the whole of humanity will witness a new world order that is far beyond imagination; everyone will benefit to the extent which their nature, disposition and mentality allow.

THE INHERITORS OF THE EARTH

T he world is floating away as it spins into its real orbit… but are the rightful "inheritors of the Earth" ready to retake and restore the inheritance that has been snatched from their hands? The initial rights were granted a gift and, as such, are different from the rights acquired by effort and action. Rights that are not served for on account of due merit, even if initially given to a particular group, cadre or nation, can always be withdrawn; they may even continue to change hands among those whose portion of worthiness is greater than others, until those who are genuinely worthy have been raised up.

> Indeed We wrote in the Psalms after the Message (Torah) that My servants, the righteous, shall inherit the Earth. (Anbiya 21: 105)

Without doubt that promise, guaranteed in this verse by an oath, will be fulfilled one day. Nor, without doubt, is it the inheritance of the Earth only; for inheriting the Earth also means governing and managing the resources of the sky and space. It will be almost a universal "dominion." As this dominion is one that will be deputed to a regent or steward on behalf of the Lord, it is extremely important, indeed essential, that the attributes that are appropriate to inheriting the Earth and the heavens are conformed to. Indeed, only so far as the required attributes are realized and practiced can the dream come true.

Since in troubled times of history those who had a claim to be the inheritors, but who failed to carry out the duties required by this heavenly inheritance, were deprived of it by the true

Owner of the dominion; the only way for them to be saved from such deprivation is to return and take refuge in submission to Him.

God did not promise this inheritance to a particular clan, tribe, nation, or race. The inheritance is for those of His servants who are righteous in thought and religion; for those who have a *Muhammadi* spirit and Qur'anic morality; who foster and retain the idea of unity, accord, togetherness, and solidarity; who are aware of the era they are living in; who are well-equipped with science and knowledge; who always keep and observe the balance between this world and the next; in short, for the heroes of spirit, spiritual reality and vision who aspire to the same orbit as the Companions of God's Messenger, the stars ornamented across the sky of prophethood. And this inheritance is within *sunnatullah*, the course of God, His way of treatment.

According to the verse, *For you shall not find any alteration in the course of God; and you shall not find any change in the course of God* (Fatir 35:43), this is a law of nature, that is a law of creation as ordained by the Creator, and it is immutable.

That is why becoming the inheritors of the Earth is conditional, first and foremost, on striving to live the religion in line with the Qur'an and Sunna. Secondly, it means striving to make religion soul of life. Thirdly, it is conditional to be deserving heirs of the science and knowledge of the era. The point that should never be forgotten is that the punishment falls inevitably upon those who do not abide by the natural laws operating in the universe (the manifestations of God's Will and Power in the universe) and the Divine laws (as manifested in divine scriptures which are derived from God's attribute of *kalam*—speaking to the humanity), in the revealed scriptures. This punishment also falls upon those who have suffered a negative change in their spiritual life, even though they may be, at the time, enjoying the dominion of rule over the rest. History, the graveyard of nations that have declined and become extinct for that reason, attests to this fact. God never withdraws the bounties He has granted to a society or nation and never makes them change, unless they themselves implement changes in their living, inner world, unless they deform themselves, their souls and essence. The verse cited above and the following—*Verily, God does not change the condition of a people until they change that which is within themselves* (Rad 13:11)—which concerns rule and being ruled, honor and humiliation, reminds us of a significant general principle and also highlights the particular failing of contemporary Muslims.

We can summarize this failing as the deformation that is suffered in both their inner structure (in their hearts and souls) and in their outward structure (their falling behind in contemporary knowledge). It does not much matter whether this is the result of the obstacles and impediments placed by the outside world over two hundred years, or from their own ignorance, weaknesses, inabilities and deficiencies. One thing is certain, namely that the Islamic community is losing blood on account of its indifference to, and want of interest in, the sources of power which kept it standing firm for ages and which made it the rightful "inheritor of the Earth."

Can we say of those who claim, on behalf of the Muslim community, to represent Islam at such unfortunate times that they have the profound life of heart and soul that the first Muslims had? Can we say that Muslims leave aside and forget their own desires to live and instead have the desire and spiritual resolve to make others live? Again, how many people can we point to now who live with the awareness of whether what they are doing will lead to good, loftier, more valuable and beneficial things or status, or whether it will lead to destruction? How many sincere people can we point to who prefer to pass away honorably rather than to live on despised? How many bright souls can we show who have never given in to the pressures of the obstacles and enemies in front of them and who have continued to live without changing their course and direction?

During such unfortunate periods, the weakness of the administration and the administrators is literally heart-breaking. Although the Qur'an forbids Muslims to live under the rule of tyrants, unfortunately we have been unable to save ourselves from this. Alas, we cannot deny that we have been suffering great misery and humiliation under oppressors who have been crushing us for years under their domination.

The truth of the matter is that we have committed one of the most unforgivable errors of history: just to make our world materially prosperous, we have sacrificed our religion to the world and adopted a system of thought which has made the world preferable to religion; subsequently we have been struggling in "a web of impossibilities and absurdities." Consequently, not only have we lost religion, we have also failed to gain the world. This glorious but unfortunate nation suffered a period of emptying: a blessed history and a thousand-year heritage were rejected; artificial, newly-invented origins was imposed upon the people; a great state was re-designed on blocks of inflated principles that have no enduring value; history, associations of community and culture, ancestry, and national culture and heritage were despised, insulted and derided; we took refuge with those who had for a thousand years opposed our system of thought and with their alien ideas; these were thereby imported into our country along with the most profane ideas and dire expressions. Those who successfully uttered and praised such things in prose and poetry were showered with awards and prizes; in a complete world of the wronged, unjustly treated, condemned and oppressed, they went almost as far as communism in an attempt to prosper in feelings, thought, and morality.

I can still recollect that when ideologies like socialism and communism were in their heyday there was a group of almost a dozen incompetents disabled by unbelief who doubted even themselves and who always felt the need to hide behind public figures, dogmas, and ideologies in order to attack religion and assault the sacred things in a crude and vulgar fashion. At the present time we are experiencing a most dreadful and disgraceful campaign of the same sort by the very same individuals, the same gang. Still based on and backed up by the same illegitimate ideologies, they spew out their hatred, malice, and rancor and all but declare war in their effort to silence the devout, religious people and the religious life. Turkish national poet laureate, M. Akif Ersoy (1873-1936), the writer of the Turkish National Anthem, has dealt with such issues in his corpus, *Safahat* (Stages), in heartfelt bitterness and mental anguish, where he has impressively expressed the darkest period when Muslims and Islam were put under surveillance, chased, persecuted, and prosecuted, and when the love and enthusiasm for and attachment to religion were disgraced, extinguished, and exterminated.

However, I must point out that this noble nation, which has been compelled to suffer blasphemous and arbitrary oppressions for years, has never been completely subdued, and the aspirations to the eternal life in its thoughts have never been extinguished. These thoughts are at the same time a red hot ember, a spark that crackles with life when it stirs, and a source of light which is able to illuminate the worlds; it has so far been compacted with the centripetal force of caution, circumspection, foresight, and composure that it is reduced in size, fitting into a seed, and thus is able to survive the most calamitous days of the century, reaching forward to the horizon of fulfilling its purpose, and waiting in readiness to fully enlighten the world when its time comes.

We should take the long period of desolation to the same degree as hardships endured and effort exerted. By understand-

ing Islam, which is a sufficient source of power for our material and spiritual revival, according to its essence, and by joining
with the righteous servants, whose emotions, thoughts, perceptions, consciousness, and willpower are sound and strong, who
stand firm and upright with the thought of living and communicating God's Word,[4] who are systematic in the acquisition of
knowledge, trustworthy in their work and attitudes, of upright
character, who would not give in to sensual desires, and who
have managed to harmonize their hearts and minds, let us prove
once more that we are the inheritors of the Earth.

If God grants His guidance and success to us we would like
to continue our journey in the direction of this lost line.

ON HOW TO FIND OUR PATH

Since the day we were deprived of the inheritance of the Earth, the Islamic world has been in a heart-breaking plight, trapped between the weaknesses of the Muslims and the ruthless assaults of its enemies. Wrong, injustice, and oppression may be the signs of the aggressors, but the weaknesses of the Muslims are unacceptable. When the Messenger of God said, "O my Lord, I take refuge in you from the intrepidity of the sinners and from the weakness of the God-fearing" he was most probably referring to this fact.

The fact that Muslim thought and reasoning were shaken and interrupted, that it stagnated and putrefied meant that the Muslims were misdirected, turned away from the straight path which takes its direction from the Qur'an and which orbits around the Prophet. This decay overshadowed the universality of Islam and prevented this universal religion from fulfilling its function. Clearly such deviation, which has become chronic among the Muslims of recent centuries and especially among Muslim leaders, cannot be eradicated by the establishment of a few schools, panels, and conferences. Nor can it even be fully understood in the course of a few ephemeral, fleeting speeches, lectures, and proposals.

To eradicate this long-standing deviation, whose roots go back some several centuries and which is supported by the erroneous use of science and technology today, requires that we rediscover ourselves, find and know who we are, and reacquaint ourselves with Islamic consciousness and styles of thought and reasoning; it requires long-term effort, determined zeal, sufficient time, ceaseless patience, vigorous hope, unshakeable willpower and constant composure. If, however, we cannot find our own style and continue to seek a way out other than the very pit into which we have fallen, we will have both deceived ourselves and disappointed our generations once more.

In view of this, there is an obligation for us to realize conception in order to view creation and events from the Islamic perspective and to examine everything with Islamic reasoning. To achieve this, our knowledge about humanity, life, and the universe should first be sound and in accord with the essence and reality of matter, on the same course and orbit as its origin and objectives; all its parts should support one another and collaborate; the whole and the parts should be related or interconnected, like different voices expressing the same theme, like a composition with a single rhythm and meter, like a central embroidered motif encircled by a repeating pattern. Every phenomenon or thing should be perceived and known as being in one way or another essentially and significantly interconnected with every other thing and with its surroundings. Second, since all things, beings, and phenomena in the universe are full of worlds of meaning, content, and wisdom, indeed, series, systems, or compositions of wisdom, like a book which is open to all beings and events, a dazzling, multifaceted masterpiece full of profundities, reflecting and manifesting innumerable Divine works, reason and understanding should be employed to understand all these things and events, to comprehend the relationships between the smaller parts without becoming entangled in trivialities. Instead, by remaining aware of the general and the universal which lie behind and in the singular and particular, while venturing on into the general and universal in order to include the remotest areas of details and particulars we may be able to ensure that some parts of our work and studies, our proofs and confirmations, and differences of periods and times do not contradict, negate, or quash other parts.

This should not be understood to mean that specialization or departmentalization should be ignored. Of course, each of us should specialize in our own field, strive for excellence in that career and achieve the desired objectives in our own area of work. However, while doing this, the meaning, content, status, and in particular, the aim and objectives of the whole should not be neglected. These should be realized in whatever way is appropriate, be it via a collective consciousness or by its proper channeling along with knowledge, or through excellent coordination, or by genius. There is no doubt that we are in need of such a universal (holistic) and comprehensive (inclusive) perspective, as well as a general and objective evaluation.

Today we are in great need, above all else, of an objective mind which can see yesterday and today together, which can take humanity, life, and the universe into its perspective all at the same time, which can draw comparisons, which is receptive to the dimensions of the causes of and reasons for existence, which is cognizant of the scenarios of the rise, continuance, and fall of nations and communities, which can judge the errors, faults, and merits of sociology and psychology, which is alert to the rise, decline, and death in the cycles of civilizations, which has skill, sound conscience, and integrity to distinguish means and ends, which is respectful of the objectives and familiar with the principles and wisdom of the Divine Law and purposes of the Lawgiver (the Prophet), which is knowledgeable about the essentials which are accepted as basis for religious decrees and which is open to the thoughts and inspirations that emanate from God.

While we are clearing and releasing the blocked channels of our thought, and realigning our system of reasoning, which has turned away from the sublime and thus become stale, so that it travels in its proper orbit around the Qur'an, we will not neglect the secrets of humanity, life, and the universe. As well as acting minutely upon the religious commands and making them part of life, an act which is one of the most significant bases of a long and uninterrupted continuance, we must smooth the way as the Messenger of God made it easy, with kindness and gentleness, and with tolerance and forbearance, showing it to be a path of encouragement which invites with glad tidings, rather than one which discourages and repels with disgust and aversion.

We must put the power of knowledge and contemplation at the disposal of Islam and Islamic interpretation and thus bring to an end the barrenness and unproductiveness of recent centuries. We must establish everywhere, in homes and streets, in schools and places of worship, observatories from which the truth behind humanity, life, and the universe can be seen.

We must reopen the routes to eternity which have been blocked for some centuries. We must raise Islam to the first and most important point on the agenda, one that is to be dwelt on in every element of life.

We must become sensitive to the issue of cause and effect and so act rationally and calculatedly, according to the principle of the relation and proportion of causes. Such a quality of understanding, perception, comprehension, and maturity will facilitate our renewal and reformation and provide us with the foundation stones on which to base an eternal life.

Some may think that attaching so much importance to causes is impertinent. To some extent I agree. However, humanity must do what it is obliged to do and must not interfere with what the Divine work requires. A duty is our responsibility, and to have recourse to causes in the fulfillment of that duty is a form of entreaty or petition presented at the door of God's mercy, equivalent to a prayer made in order to obtain a desired outcome. To accept that this is so is a prerequisite of acknowledging the fact that we are the created and He is the Creator, and of acknowledging His Divine Attributes.

However, there is the other side of the coin. God grants to us free will (whose existence is considered to be nominal) and accepts it as an invitation to His Will and Willpower, and promises to establish the most essential projects upon this will, a plan He has implemented and continue to do so. God created our will as an occasion of merit or sin, and as a basis for recompense and punishment, and accepts it as an agent for ascribing to good and evil.

In the light of the consequences ascribed to it, God ascribes to our will which has no value in itself, a value above all values, such that had He not done so, life would have ceased, human beings would have been reduced to inanimate things, the laying of obligations on God's servants would have become pointless, and everything would have been reduced to futility, uselessness, and absurdity. This is why God attaches importance to our will and to the desires and wishes of humanity; He accepts it as a condition for the construction and prosperity of both this world and the Hereafter, making it a considerable cause, like a magical switch to a powerful electrical mechanism that can illuminate the worlds. In the same way He can create and give existence to an ocean from a drop, a sun from an atom, and whole worlds from nothingness, and thus manifests one of the mysterious dimensions of His power.

Neither cause nor anything else rules, governs, or exerts influence on God, the All-Mighty Creator. Nothing binds His Divine Will and Power. All is decreed and God is the one and the only, the absolute Ruler. Yet observation of the causes, ascribing effects to them, and evaluating the reasons for effects as the slight and minor parts of agency is God's command too. Therefore, when people do not observe the principles of the laws of nature created by God, called "*Sunnatullah*" (the way of

God's doing / the course of God, the way of His treatment), we believe that they will fail to a great extent in this world and to a certain extent in the Hereafter as well.

How meaningful was the approach of Caliph 'Umar when avoiding a plague-stricken area; he said to those who were unable to reconcile his flight with the idea of resignation to one's fate and submission to one's lot, "I am running from God's Will back to God's Will again."

In one's actions, activities, work, and endeavors, being heedlessly result-oriented, making those results the sole object of one's wishes, and unnecessarily being overburdened is both a kind of suffering and impertinence, as if, may God forbid, one is bargaining with God. On the other hand, disregarding human choice and willpower and expecting the result to come by wonderful, almost miraculous means, in an extraordinary way, directly from God, is a strange fancy, an illusion, and an excuse for wretchedness. The Qur'an says many times in many chapters *"as a reward for what they did," "as a reward for what they earned,"* or *"as a recompense for what they committed."*

The Qur'an warns people that what they have experienced and what they will enjoy or suffer of good or evil is a result of their own behavior, actions, and deeds. When the Messenger of God, the perfect example of the balance of heart, mind, and conscience, said "On the day of Judgment, without having an opportunity to take a step, man will be questioned of where he passed his lifetime, how he used his knowledge, how he gained his wealth and where he spent it, and where he wore out his body," he pointed out the strong and mysterious relation between cause and effect, effort and gain.

While Islam, through the Qur'an and Sunna, regulates a believer's faith and actions, prayers and morality, and their life in this world and the next, it whispers at the same time, between the lines, into our world of the mind, heart, soul, emotions, conscience, and consciousness from a realm of other dimensions, the worlds of the beyond, such different things that heavenly breezes are produced in the depths of our personality and divine-colored emotions. In this way, at every instant, Islam revives humanity once more in a different dimension.

Thus we find ourselves in the position of vicegerency to God, in a position to intervene in natural phenomena, and in a position to comprehend and examine the mysteries of the laws of nature. Then we are able to perceive the book of the universe, which comes from the Divine Will and Power, and the declarations which flow from His divine attribute of Kalam (Speech) through revelation, as the two sides of one unity and we can regulate our thoughts and conceptions, acts and attitudes, our considerations of this world and the Hereafter according to the balance in the Earth and heavens.

Islam weaves its warp and weft through the mind, body, soul, and conscience of humanity, intertwining the dimensions of this world and the Hereafter into a rich and colorful lacework. Turn by turn the threads of the mind, body, soul, or conscience are laid over and under each other, but none of them by itself is able to reflect and represent Islam, nor can any of them by themselves express Islam in its true sense and completeness.

Islam, the All-Mighty Creator's greatest and universal gift to all, can be carried to real life by the humanity, the spiritual index of all creation, first and foremost by His favor, by that which is made from the intellect, conscience, soul, body, and the inner fine qualities of soul. We will expand on this in the coming sections.

TOWARD TOMORROW

For centuries now the Islamic world has squirmed in the vicious grasp of error and has remained unable to turn for succor in any way to its own spirit and essence. Whenever it has broken free and succeeded in taking two steps forward, it has immediately taken several steps back and lost itself in the byways. Such whimsical wandering or deliberate deviation, in which there is more harm than good and in which the harmful sweeps away the beneficial, hinders society's efforts to seek and find itself within itself and deeply disturbs the work done and the people who do it. We have seen everything in this wide world deteriorate beyond recovery and the wheels of the states and nations turn against their own selves.

Therefore we believe in the necessity to investigate the Islamic world with its understanding of faith, its own acceptance and interpretation of Islam, its consciousness of the Divine, its zeal and yearning, its reason, logic, mode and system of thinking, its style of expressing and communicating itself, and its own institutions, which will make humanity acquire these attributes and skills. In this way we may direct our world to a thorough renewal in all its aspects and elements.

The fundamentals of our spiritual life are religious thought and imagination. Not only have we sustained our life with these, but we have also taken action by relying on them. If we were to be parted from them, we would find ourselves a thousand years back. Religion is not only an assemblage of rituals and worship, its goals include giving meaning to humanity and the universe, becoming open to human nature in its essence and spirit, realizing the desires which go beyond this world, and responding to the intimations of eternity in human conscience. Religion embraces the whole of individual and collective life; it intervenes in everything we have of mind, heart, and soul; it gives its tincture to all our acts according to our intentions, and imbues everything with its color.

The axis of every act of a believer is worship, every striving has a dimension of the struggle against one's carnal desires— greater jihad—and every effort is directed at the Hereafter and seeking God's pleasure. There is no separation of this world and the next in the believer's life: there are no obstructions between the mind and the heart; the believer's emotions are always united with their reason, and their inspirations are not ignored by their judgment. So, in their mental world, experience is a ladder made of light, stretching up to the mind; knowledge is a high bastion, reinforced with understanding, wisdom, and intuition. The believer is an eagle, continuously soaring to infinity on the giant wings of love; they are the embosser who embosses all existence with their stamp and mallet of intelligence on that bastion. There can be found no gap in any place in such an understanding, nor is there any neglect of humanity, either individually or collectively.

Those who perceive religion as being contradictory to science and reason are the afflicted; they are unaware of the spirit of both religion and reason. Moreover, it is absolutely fraudulent to hold religion responsible for clashes between different sections of society. Conflicts between peoples and groups of people arise from ignorance, from ambition for personal advantage and profit, or from the vested interests of particular groups, parties, or classes. Religion neither approves nor condones such qualities and ambitions. In fact, there are conflicts and clashes between some religious individuals, but this is because, even though they have the same spirit, they do not hold the same degree of belief, they cannot preserve sincerity; sometimes they cannot overcome their feelings and are defeated by them. Otherwise, virtue with faith cannot approve of nor lead to such calamities. Indeed, the only way to avoid falling into such misfortunes is to establish religion with all its institutions within our daily life so that it becomes the life-blood of society as a whole.

The Islamic community needs a resurrection; it needs a serious reform in its mental, spiritual, and intellectual faculties. To use a more positive expression, it needs to be revived, combining serious efforts to preserve the original principles of the religion with extensiveness and universality as far as permitted by the flexibility of the divine decrees, so that it meets the needs of people from all walks of life, in all places and times, and so that it embraces the whole of life.

Since the advent of Islam—and may God never cause us to be deprived of its shelter—this blessed system has opened its doors to renewals many times, and experienced many revivals. Schools of doctrine (*madhhab*) in general, certainly the great majority of them, represent new developments in the fields of jurisprudence and law; the religious Sufi orders worked on the paths to heart and soul and turned them into broad highways; schools and colleges, during the times when they functioned properly, were mostly occupied with making sense of the universe and the beings in it. As to the renewal and revival hoped for in the present time, it must be the combination of all these; it will be possible only by bringing all these together, by leaving off the outward molds for the inner core, leaving off the outward forms for the soul—that is, by turning to certainty in faith, sincerity in deeds, and God-consciousness in thought and feeling.

Quantity in acts of worship should be complete and quality should be the goal: words should be the means of the prayer and the soul and sincerity are essential; the Sunna should be the guide and consciousness is a necessity. In all of these God should be the goal. The prescribed daily prayers are not a set of physical exercises of sitting up and bending down; giving alms is not giving up a small tax on one's income or goods to allay the misfortunes of some unknown people in unknown places for unknown purposes; fasting is not dieting or merely abstaining from eating or drinking; and pilgrimage, the hajj, is not traveling from one town to another to spend one's savings in a foreign currency in a different country. If all these acts are not performed within their own axis and courses and spirit, how are they different from comparable mundane activities? Concentrating on quantity in acts of worship can only be a childish game; crying out and yelling without spirit in one's petitions is for those who are looking only to exercise their vocal cords; going on pilgrimage while unaware of its essence is only an effort to comfort oneself with the title of pilgrim and some anecdotes of the journey. How can one make sense of acts of worship performed in that way?

The way not to waste away in the web of such negatives is by mobilizing to raise the "physicians of the soul and essential reality" which can fill the vacuum in us, eradicate our weaknesses, rescue us from being slaves to our body and carnal desires, and direct us to the level of the life of the heart and soul. We need physicians of the soul and reality whose hearts are open to all fields of all knowledge: perspicacity, culture, spiritual knowledge, inspirations and divine blessings, abundance and prosperity, enlightenment; from physics to metaphysics, from mathematics to ethics, from chemistry to spirituality, from astronomy to subjectivism, from fine arts to Sufism, from law to jurisprudence, from politics to special training of religious Sufi orders: journeying and initiation in Sufi terms). We are not in need of this or that particular quality or ability, but rather the whole comprehensive mind. Just as the brain has connections and interactions with all the parts and cells of a body, from the nearest to the farthest, from the smallest to the biggest, by means of nerve fibers, so too will such a cadre of minds be connected, communicating and interacting with the atoms, molecules and particles of the nation-body. So will it reach all the units and organs that constitute society. So will its hand be in and over the vital institutions. So will it convey gently, to everyone in all walks of life, certain things from the soul and reality, which come from the past and gain more depth with the present and stretch into the future.

Such a cadre of physicians of the soul will embrace all, from the attentive and well-behaved children in school to those idling on the streets, and by conveying the messages of their soul to all of them, and by elevating them to the level of people who have knowledge, skills, and genius for the future, they will present them for the common good and benefit of society. In all student houses, hostels, schools, institutions of higher education, and places of repose, worship, and spiritual enlightenment, they will purify everyone, from all sections and levels of society, of the foulness of the age, and channel them to human perfection.

Moreover, this cadre will tame the powerful weapons of the media, such as newspapers, journals, the radio and television, and will make them the voice and breath of national and religious life, and through these media, they will teach the owners of the darkest feelings, thoughts, and voices ways to become human.

Moreover, this cadre will save our institutions of education and training, which now change their forms and directions according to internal deviations and foreign pressures, which sway with the wind from the command and control of others, and will make them instead open and responsive to the requirements of the present, re-ordering and organizing them according to historical perspectives, and raising them by use of styles, methodologies, and a high-standard of planning, to be places of great quality and purpose.

Thus, in sum, we will rise from the misery of rigid and empty formalism to true scientific understanding; from dignifying diverse vile and disgraceful works with the title of "art" to true art and aesthetics; from customs, addictions, and obsessions of unknown origin to the consciousness of a morality based on history and religion; from the snares of various gnawing thoughts in our hearts to the oneness of service, submission, consciousness, as well as resignation and reliance in God.

The world experiences this rush of reformations. However, we do not believe that anything new will emerge from the tatters of capitalism, or the fantasy of communism, or the debris of socialism, or the hybrids of social democracy, or old-fashioned liberalism. The truth of the matter is if there is a world open to a new world order, it is our world. Coming generations, looking back, will probably consider it our "Renaissance."

This revival will make our feelings and horizons of thought, and also of understanding of art and aesthetics, gain depth and variety greater than it has had until now. In this way we will find our own aesthetic pleasures, reach our own music, and discover our own romanticism. By establishing our own people on a strong foundation in every field, from science to art, from thought to morality, we will secure their future.

In this matter, effort and dynamism will be our banner, and consciousness of faith and truth will be our source of strength. Those who have made us wander from door to door and who have expected remedies or solutions from faithlessness and immorality have always been wrong. We have always acquired honor and remained honorable as long as we have held fast to and surrendered to God whole-heartedly, and as long as we have preferred our nation, people and land, in whose bosom we have thrived, to anything in the world. I assume it is not necessary to explain the alternative...

THE WORLD WE LONG FOR

In many different eras, in many different parts of the world, many have stepped forward with claims of reformations and reconstructions under different names and titles. Such claims have always been controversial, with one exception which embraces the whole of creation, the veiled reality beyond, the humanity, and life. This is undoubtedly our world, especially across a wide span of its lifetime.

After long ages of crises and depressions, despite all odds, this nation is still capable of such a regeneration; it still has the potential to realize a new resurrection, and it has accumulated sufficient knowledge to guide all the new formations around it. Moreover, it has the advantage of the subconscious acceptance by the peoples which shared history, a leadership which may possibly be of use again in the future. It is complete and sufficient with all it represents, as long as it can use once more the driving forces which were the soul and life-blood of such a long and magnificent past, in the proper time and place.

Once, in almost all the sciences, both natural and religious, our nation walked far ahead of its age. These sciences ranged from Sufism (*tasawwuf*) to logic, from urban planning to aesthetics, and were embodied in the geniuses who studied phenomena minutely, such as Khwarizmi, Biruni, Ibn Sina (Avicenna), and Zahrawi; in masters of law and Islamic jurisprudence such as Abu Hanifa, Imam Muhammad, Sarakhsi, and Marginani; in the talents who surpassed human norms and defeated logic with logic and heart and lived their lives conscientiously, such as Imam Ghazali, Razi, Mawlana Jalal al-Din

Rumi, Shaykh-Naqshband; in the heroes of reasoning and intelligence, such as Imam Maturidi, Taftazani, Sayyid Sharif and Dawwani; and in artistic geniuses such as the architects Hayreddin and Sinan, Itri and Dede Efendi. Now, by mobilizing all its bright minds and souls, our nation may shortly realize a second or third renaissance. Starting from the recognition of the soul and essence of Islam, and by reaching toward the re-interpretation of all existence, from the boundless divine climates of sufi path to universal metaphysics; from Islamic self-accounting and self-supervision to the vigilance, circumspection, and self-possession which make man gain lofty values; from the cities and urbanization, in which our inner world takes repose and where we can breathe, to the aesthetics which will be the property of all; from the art which embroiders the essence and reality everywhere and seeks infinity in all it embroiders to the true pleasures of aesthetics, which becomes more and more other-worldly, more and more refined and integrates with the beyond, by all these means, this nation can open a new chapter. However, such a great task is not accomplished lightly...

For so many years, our spiritual life has to a great extent been extinguished; our religious world has become dysfunctional; the tongues of our hearts have been tied by making people forget intense, love (*ashq*) and ecstasy (*wajd*); we have perverted all minds which read and think into a hard positivism; bigotry has been installed in the place of firmness of character, strength of religion, and perseverance in truth; even in asking for the Hereafter and paradise, with a distorted mentality, petitioners have in mind some continuation of the ordinary happiness in this world. It is therefore impossible to open a new chapter without ripping such misdirected, deep-rooted thoughts and ideas out of ourselves.

This does not mean that the foulnesses that have sullied our souls for ages cannot be eradicated. However, without ridding ourselves of the urges and sentiments which are the true reasons for the fall and dissolution of our people, such as greed, laziness, ambition for fame, yearning for status, selfishness, and worldly-mindedness, without establishing in their place the spirit of abstinence, courage, modesty and humility, altruism, spirituality, piety and godliness—which are all of the essence and truth of Islam—without directing people to truth, without purifying and reforming them with the sense of truth, and without causing such an understanding to permeate and prevail in the society, it would be well-nigh impossible to reach the straight path and calm days.

It is not completely impossible, though. If we have heroes left among us who are loyal to the essential reality of Islam and have the willpower to embrace the age we live in and fulfill its requirements, this renewal and change will certainly take place. In fact there are such heroes present among us and it will be a transformation that is shaped by the Qur'an and tempered by the natural disposition. This will happen in such a manner that even those who are closed to such understanding, and the masses who insist on being closed to it, will not be able to prevent it. To date all renaissances worldwide have been the result of the efforts and work of the few individual geniuses who are regarded as their architects; they did not arise from the effort and movement of the masses. Just as in the years immediately following the advent of Islam, some renewals and changes were the result of, not more than a dozen exceptional souls and their intelligence and ideas, souls who were raised during the time of the Umayyads and Abbasids, so too were those vast thoughts, profound souls, and bright dispositions behind the centrifugal movements and revivals during the later periods of the Ilkhanids, Karakhanids, Seljuks and Ottomans. The ways opened by such guiding souls, who emerged with a complete spiritual awareness in almost every age, became over time schools of thought which breathed the spirit of reconstruction and reformation into the masses. Those who succeeded them also followed those guides and their thoughts, and the masses followed them and sheltered in their enlightened climate too. Such great guides became the life-blood and soul of the people and lived with them like a spirit. However, during the periods when such great minds were gone, wiped out, and when people of good standing were not raised to take their place, the whole of society became a corpse, thoughts became charred remains, and dreams of renewal became impossibilities.

Now, as the days turn to spring and dawn chases dawn, we are becoming hopeful, expectant, and praying to our Lord, "Grant us willpower supported by your Will, which will erect the statue of our souls, make our hearts as green as the slopes of the hills of Paradise, and make our souls reach the secrets of the innermost part of Your Divinity. Show our people the ways to revival in the Muhammadi line."

To ask for and expect this is our right, duty, and the natural consequence of our faith. However, while exercising this right and fulfilling this duty, we must make frequent reference to our glorious past and shelter in the values that made our past magnificent. This is the way that other civilizations have renewed themselves. As Western Europe proceeded through its Renaissance toward its present civilization, it took refuge in Christianity, took the Greeks as a model and espoused the values of ancient Rome. Provided that the same course of direction is followed, development is possible for any civilization. So, too, will we shelter in our own past and the roots of our essence and take our examples from the vastness of Divinity which time can never obscure. From philosophical thinking to the truth of Sufism, from the established view of religion to its moral dimension, we will take our models from the most enlightened, the brightest eras, of which we are always proud, and which we consider to be the golden slice of time, and we will weave the tapestry of our future, thread by thread, on the canvas of time. In this tapestry Mawlana Jalal al-Din Rumi will come together with

Taftazani, Yunus Emre will sit on the same prayer mat with Mahdumguli, Fuzuli will embrace Mehmed Akif, Uluğ Bey will salute Abu Hanifa, Hodja Dehhani will sit knee to knee with Imam Ghazali, Muhy al-Din ibn Arabi will throw roses to Ibn Sina, Imam Rabbani will be thrilled by the glad-tidings for Bediüzzaman Said Nursi. From such a great past, with its wide panorama, the men of stature will come together and whisper to us the charm of salvation and revival.

As long as we can recover our thoughts, feelings, methods, and philosophy, it will suffice to bring them together to find that heavenly and immortal style of ours. That is why, as I see it, we should first of all re-examine all the roads that we are going to take and repair and reinforce them once again. Quintessential to our renaissance are the inspiration and fruitfulness of religious zeal, a reassuring atmosphere, firmness, gravity, sobriety, and wisdom in our reasoning and logic; stability and humanism that give us the freedom to be ourselves; philosophical depth, refinement and contemplative abstraction in our arts and philosophy; and that all these should have the quality of being logical at the core and inspired by revelation.

In this renewal, the pleasure of God is the ultimate goal. The soul is positioned ahead of the body. The self (*nafs*) is an essential dynamic which will ignite the consciousness of duty under the rule of heart. The love of humanity and country is an indispensable passion. Morality, which will never be abandoned, is a vital provision for the journey. Humanity, life and the universe are a mysterious book with different chapters, whose leaves we frequently scrutinize through the lens of the Qur'an. Humanity is a significant source of power with its character and true human values. Goals and objectives must be just, fair, and sacred, and the ways leading to the goals and objectives should be indicated by the Qur'an and Sunna. These are all safeguards against error.

That which we might call a "prescription" for our salvation consists of particular points: focusing effort on the future of our people and country; expending energy on changing our unfortunate fate of the last few centuries; making the soul which will mold and form our society into the life of our corpses; turning a new page in the history of our people. These are only a few essential elements of our dream of civilization and renewal that far excels any utopia.

THE STATUE OF OUR SOULS

E
arlier I briefly outlined the attributes of the inheritors of the Earth. Now I shall clarify and expand on these attributes.

The first attribute of the inheritors is perfect faith. The Qur'an establishes that the purpose of the creation of human beings is faith in God with the horizon of knowledge, the spirit of love, the dimension of ecstatic love and joyful zeal, and the hues of spiritual pleasures. Human beings are responsible for constructing their world of faith and thought, either by establishing pathways from their own essence to the depths of existence or by taking various crosscuts from existence and assessing them within their essence. This also entails the emergence of the latent human truth in their soul. Only by the light of faith, can we perceive our essence, the depths in our essence, and the goals and objectives of existence; then we can become aware of the interior aspects of the universe and events and what is beyond. Then we can comprehend the existence within its dimensions. Unbelief is an obstructed, blocked, and choked-up system. In the eyes of an unbeliever, existence started with chaos, developed within the frightening uncertainties of coincidence, and is sliding away rapidly into a terrifying end. Within this shaky rolling and rumbling there is no breath of God's compassion to lend relief or joy to the soul, no small sheltering place for us with our human aspirations to bask safely in cool consoling breezes, not even a small foothold onto which we can step.

In contrast, a person of belief, who perceives their route and destination and their duties and responsibilities, sees everything as wholly bright and luminous; they step where they are supposed to without the least anxiety, and walk toward their destination fearlessly, confidently and securely. On their journey they investigate existence and what is beyond it innumerable times; they distil things and events countless times; they try to open every door and to seek to establish relations with every object; where their knowledge, experience, and discoveries fall short they are contented with the facts as far as they have been confirmed by themselves and others, and they press on with their journey.

By these criteria, a traveler of faith can be seen to have discovered a very significant power source. The ammunition and treasure, which is expressed in *"There is no might nor power, except with God"* and which belongs to the beyond, is such a significant source of power and light that the one who acquires it is no longer in need of any other. This person then always sees and knows Him; they rush to join His company and retinue and direct their life toward Him and according to Him; they can challenge all the worldly powers in proportion to their knowledge and trust in Him and with the hope that they can overcome everything; even under the most adverse circumstances they live in joyful zeal and never fall into pessimism.

As this point is the subject matter of works such as the *Risale-i Nur* and so many other books, I refer the readers to those works and shall now pass on to the second attribute.

The second attribute of the inheritors is "love," which is considered to be the most important elixir of revival. The person who equips and improves their heart with faith in God and knowledge of Him in proportion to that faith and knowledge, feel a profound affection and a vast love for all human beings and in fact for all creation; and thus they live their whole life in the ebbs and flows of an all-embracing love, being in a state of rapture and ecstasy, attraction, and the feeling of being attracted toward God, and spiritual pleasures. As in all periods, now it is necessary for hearts to become exuberant and enthused with love and overflowing with joyful zeal, with a new understanding in order to realize such a great revival. For without love, it is not possible to realize an effort or movement which is lasting and effective with respect to its consequences; likewise they should focus on the Hereafter. We can understand divine love as being, before God, the establishment of our place within the relations which give existence and existing to feel the pleasure of being created by Him, of our being the shadow of the light of His Being, accepting that His pleasure is the aim of the created and the reason for the creation, and being always after His love and pleasure. Such a love for God is an infinite and mysterious source of power and the inheritors of the earth should not neglect this source, but live and enjoy it fully.

The West acquainted itself with love, in its materially hued dimensions, following the philosophers and in the foggy climate of philosophy they only tasted it, but experienced doubts, indecision, suspicion and uncertainty throughout. We will look at existence and its source through the lens of the Qur'an and Sunna. By resorting and referring to the balancing principles of these two sources and setting forth for their vastness open to metaphysics, we will realize the love—the fever of love that we ignite in our hearts—for the Creator and realize the attachment we feel, just because of Him, to the whole of existence. For, within these two sources (the Qur'an and Sunna), the origin of man, his place in the universe, the aim of his existence, and the way he will follow and the end of it are so in accord with his thinking, feeling, consciousness and expectations that it is impossible not to wonder at and admire it after perceiving it to be so.

To the man of heart these two luminous sources are a rushing spring of zeal and a mine of attraction. Those who turn to them with purity and sincerity of feeling and in need will not be sent away empty-handed and those who take refuge in them do not die eternally. That suffices as long as those who refer to and take refuge in them do so with the sincerity and profundity of an Imam Ghazali, Imam Rabbani, Shah Wali or Bediüzzaman Said Nursi; as long as they approach them with the enthusiasm and excitement of Jalal al-Din Rumi, Shaykh Galip or Mehmed Akif; as long as they turn to them with the faith and action of Khalid ibn Walid, Uqba bin Nafi, Salah al-Din Ayyubi, Sultan Mehmed the Conqueror or Sultan Selim II. Blending their zeal, which overflows and embraces all times and places, with the manners, styles and methods of the contemporary age to reach the spirit of the Qur'an, which never ages but surpasses all ages, and thus to reach a universal metaphysics will constitute our second step.

The third attribute of the inheritors is "turning to science with the trio of reasoning, logic and consciousness." In an era in which mankind is being dragged along behind some dark fantasies, such a turn, which will also be a response to the general tendency in human beings, will be a significant step for the salvation of the whole of mankind. As Bediüzzaman pointed out, at the end of time mankind will turn to knowledge and science with all they have; will take all their power from learning, and might will pass once more into the hands of science; purity of speech (*fasahat*), eloquence (*balaghat*), and superior expression or rhetoric will be a subject all take interest in; that is, we will experience again an era of learning and language. Indeed, in order to clear the foggy atmosphere of the conjecture surrounding us, and then to reach the truths and the Truth of the truths, there is no other way. Overcoming the void of the last few ages, achieving fullness in skills and information, and proving ourselves once more by repairing the subconscious damage of the faint and wounded state that we have been enduring year after year, all depend on the representation and expression of science, which is made to pass through the prism of Islamic thinking. As regards the near past, as its direction and target were not defined, sometimes knowledge was mixed into positivist science, and knowledge into materialist philosophy, we had serious chaos in scientific thinking and scientists came to experience an irreparable loss of esteem. This vacuum has been of use to foreigners. They have established schools and institutions industriously in every corner of our country and injected estrangement and foreignness into our offspring by means of those educational institutions. Some members of our community placed their talented, intelligent children into those institutions, in abject humiliation, and thus hastened the estrangement and foreignness a bit more. After a while there remained nothing, neither faith nor religion in those young, inexperienced and betrayed generations. Faith and Religion were ruined and rotted away. Nation-wide we were subjected to the lavishness, the cheapness and the commonplace of egoism in thought, senses, conceptions and art. The reason why it happened so was obvious. Within those schools and institutions, without any exception, those schools to which we entrusted the minds of our young without any worries or second thoughts, American culture, French morality, and English customs and traditions, and so forth, were maintained and purveyed before science and scientific thoughts. Therefore our youth, instead of catching up with the age in which they lived by means of its science, methodologies and technology, grouped into various camps and factions, and started to play the games of Marxism, Durkheimism, Leninism and Maoism. Some consoled themselves with the dreams of Communism and the dictatorship of the proletariat, some went and sank into Freudian complexes, some lost their minds to existentialism and became entangled with Sartre, some slobbered over the sacred by quoting Marcuse, some started to waste their lives among the delirium of Camus... All of these were lived through and experienced in our country, and the so-called homes of science were responsible for nursing and nurturing such ideas and experiences. During that crisis period some voices and mouths of the darkest souls continuously blackened and slandered religion and the religious but ceaselessly brought to the fore the madness and insanities originating from the West. Certainly, it is impossible for us to forget those times and their cheap pawns. Those who prepared such circumstances to the detriment of our people and country will be remembered forever as the guilty, condemned in the collective consciousness.

Now, leaving those darkest periods aside and their stewards alone with their evil acts and states, which still turn our stomachs and pain our hearts, we would like to talk about the workers of thoughts who will construct our future.

By means of scientific thinking and understanding, as we realized long ago, long before the West did, we must immerse and imbue our younger generations with science and ideas, and thus realize our revival, our Renaissance. The affliction and pain of the unfortunate destiny of the past felt in the collective conscience, the exasperations and palpitations produced by the years of foreign domination, and the reactions the negligence and exploitation of the last few ages cause in our people still raise laments like those of the Prophet Adam, groanings like those of the Prophet Jonah, and sufferings and moanings like those of the Prophet Job. After such sighs and wailings, thoughts, feelings, and efforts, and guided by historical experience and what the outcomes of the efforts and events indicate, we feel that time and distance have started to shrink and the anticipated days are not so far away, in fact just a few steps away.

The fourth attribute of the inheritors is the "action of revising their perspectives on man, life and the universe and assessing and criticizing their own rights and wrongs." We will look at three points in this regard:

a. The universe is a book which is displayed by the Creator before the eyes of man to be referred to frequently. Man is a lens open to observe the depths of existence, and a transparent index of all worlds. Life is a manifestation, the assumption of forms, of the meanings which are filtered from that book and index, and is the reflection of that which reverberates from the Divine discourse. If man, life and the universe are considered to be different on account of their outward forms and colors when these are but various faces of the same truth—and that is the reality—then their separation from one another ruins the harmony of the truth, which is a wrong, an injustice and disrespect toward man and existence.

As it is an obligation to read, understand, obey and submit to the Word of God, which comes from His divine attribute of Speech, so it is an indispensable essential to know and understand God in the entirety of things and events, which He planned by his Knowledge and created by His Divine Will and Power, and then to seek for and confirm conformity and congruity in all things and events. The Qur'an came also from God's attribute of Speech; it is the soul of all existence and the sole source of happiness. The book of the universe is the body of this truth and a very important dynamic of this world directly and of the other world indirectly with respect to the various branches of science it includes and represents. That is why understanding of and transferring these two books into practice and organizing the whole of life in accordance with them merits reward; and neglecting, ignoring, and even being unable to interpret and apply them to life merits punishment.

b. The true depth of a human should be sought in the sense, thoughts and character of a person. Likewise, that person's credit, esteem and value in the eyes of people and God, should be sought in the same. The superior human attributes, the profundity of sense and thought, and the firmness of character, are like a note of credit-worthiness or reference letter which is accepted everywhere. One who taints his faith and understanding with thoughts and attributes like those of the unbelievers, who causes anxiety and fright around him because of his character, can never attain the help and favors of the Truth, nor is it possible for him to retain his credit, esteem and trust in the eyes of people. For people and God Almighty judge individuals by their human attributes and superior characters, and reward them accordingly. That is why those who are poor in human attributes and weak in their characters can hardly achieve great things and sustain those achievements, though they appear to be good believers. On the other hand, those who are some steps ahead in firm character and superior human attributes can hardly fail altogether, even though they may not appear to be good Muslims. Just as God's appreciation, dispensation, and reward are according to one's attributes, a friendly welcome or acceptance by human beings is to some extent dependent on this too.

c. The means to attain a lawful and right target must also be lawful and right. For those who are on the Islamic line, that the object of their efforts in every enterprise should be lawful is a right, and lawfulness of the means to reach that right is an obligation. As the pleasure of God and union with the Truth cannot be acquired without sincerity and being for the sake of God, so service to Islam and the direction of Muslims to the true goals or targets cannot be achieved by evil ways and means. Quite the opposite of this seems to be true; those who have lost the favor of God Almighty and people's favorable inclination toward them by consuming their value, credit and esteem in vain, invalid, false ways cannot be expected to be successful for long.

The fifth attribute of the inheritors is being able to think freely and being respectful to freedom of thought. Being free and enjoying freedom are a significant depth of human willpower and a mysterious door through which man may set forth into the secrets of the self. One unable to set forth into that depth and unable to pass through that door can hardly be called human. For a long time we have been writhing in the terrible shackles of slavery which have subjected our thoughts and feelings to various strains coming from both inside and outside. In circumstances in which restrictions have been imposed on reading, thinking, feeling and living, it is impossible to retain one's human faculties, let alone achieve renewal and progress. In such a situation it is quite difficult to maintain even the level of a plain and common man, let alone to raise great personalities who leap with the spirit of renewal and reform, and whose eyes are on infinity. In such conditions there exist only weak characters who experience deviations in their personalities and men of sluggish souls and paralyzed senses. In our recent past distorted, deviated views and unsound, defective criteria were pumped into our souls from homes, streets, educational institutions and circles of art to the detriment of everything, from the material to the immaterial, from physics to metaphysics. During those years, we would express our obsessions while we supposed we were thinking; we would plan everything ego-centrically while never reckoning that there might be other views, beliefs and understandings beside ours; as soon as we found the opportunity, we would turn to might and with brute force administer punitive measures against right and free-will; we were always persecuting and bullying someone. It is a great pity that even now it is impossible for us to say that such things no longer happen and will not happen again. However, as we draw toward renewal, it is imperative that we should review the historical dynamics of the last thousand years and question the changes and transformations of the last one hundred and fifty years of our past. It is imperative because judgments and decisions are nowadays made according to certain unquestioned taboos.

Certain views which govern these decisions render them invalid and defective and can never be productive and can never ever prepare the awaited bright future. If it were prepared within the current understanding, clashes of the masses within the deadly web of ambitions, melees between the political parties, fights between the nations, and skirmishes between the powers would result. This is the reason today why one section of society clashes with another, why the differences turn into fights, and is the reason for the overwhelming terror, brutality and bloodshed in the world. Had it not been for the egoism, greed, ambition, and ruthlessness of humans, the world most probably would have been different from its present state.

That is why, as we are drawing toward different worlds, taking both our own attitudes to others and our own selves and ambitions into account, we have to be more free-thinking and free-willed. We need those vast hearts who can embrace impartial free-thinking, who are open to knowledge, sciences and scientific research, and who can perceive the accord between the Qur'an and *Sunnatullah* in the vast spectrum from the universe to life. In the past individual geniuses undertook and carried out these great tasks. Today, however, they can only be fulfilled by a community which takes upon itself the missions of such men of genius. As everything has become so detailed, particularized, specified, and enumerated, these tasks now assume such forms that even unique, outstanding individuals cannot accomplish them by themselves. That is why the place of genius has been now replaced by collective consciousness with consultative and collective decision-making and social conscience, which is the summary of the sixth attribute of the inheritors.

It is a fact that in the recent past the Islamic community did not possess such an understanding. In fact, it was not possible to implement collective consciousness, consultative-collective decision-making, collective mind and conscience when the schools were only spelling out their particular dogmas; colleges were dealing with only a few superficial aspects of life; dervish lodges were totally buried in metaphysics; and barracks were posturing and roaring of "might." During that period schools remained under the influence of narrow scholasticism and breathed in and out in its air; colleges were closed to science and thought, deprived of their capacity to develop and lived as if paralyzed; dervish lodges consoled themselves with anecdotes of the past instead of zeal; those who represented power felt falsely that they were forgotten and suffered from a constant need to remind others of and to prove their power. Therefore, everything became upset and the tree of the nation was shaken and almost uprooted from the ground. Unfortunately it seems that we may go on experiencing similar shakes till the day those awaited fortunate people employ the right dynamics in the right time and right place, remove the blockages between mind and heart, and establish the corridors of thought and inspiration in the esoteric dimension of humanity.

The seventh of the attributes of the inheritors is "mathematical thinking." In the past the people in Central Asia and later on in the West achieved their renaissances by means of the laws of mathematical thinking. Man discovered and brought to light many uncertain and unknown things in the mysterious world of numbers. Without going to the extremes of the Hurufis,[5] what we say is that without mathematics it is not possible to understand the relations of humanity and natural phenomena with one another. It illuminates our roads like light on the line that stretches from the universe to life; it indicates to us what is beyond the human horizon, even the depths of the world of contingencies, which is very difficult to think upon; and it makes us meet with our ideals.

On the other hand, being mathematical does not mean knowing everything related to mathematics. It is to think mathematically, to think within mathematical laws, and to be aware that it permeates everything from man's thoughts to the depths of existence, from physics to metaphysics, from matter to energy; from body to soul, from law to Sufism. In order to comprehend existence completely, we have to accept a dual method of Sufi thinking and scientific research. The West essentially lacks essence, and has tried to compensate for this loss, as far as it can, by taking refuge in mysticism. In our world, which has been always intimate with the soul of Islam, there is no need to look for anything strange or foreign, or to take refuge in anything. We have all our sources of power within our system of thought and faith. That suffices as long as we comprehend that source and spirit with its original richness. Then we will see some of the mysterious relations in existence, how harmoniously such relations run, and reach a different knowledge of observing and taking pleasure in everything.

This is only a brief summary or introduction to mathematical thinking. Even though it may seem vague and a waste of words at the present, I believe that it will have great echoes in the future.

The eighth of the attributes is our understanding of art. However, due to certain considerations at present, I will say, "Some circles are not ready yet to set out such a journey within our criteria, leave it to sometime in the future."

CONSULTATION

For the heirs of today, consultation (*shura*) is a vital attribute and an essential rule, just as it was for the first heirs. According to the Qur'an, it is the clearest sign of a believing community and the most important characteristic of a congregation who have given their hearts to Islam. The importance of consultation is mentioned in the Qur'an to the same degree as *salat* (prescribed prayers) and *infaq* (giving to maintain the religion and people for the sake of God):

> . . . Those who hearken to their Lord, and establish regular prayer, who conduct their affairs by mutual consultation, who spend out of what We have bestowed upon them for sustenance. (Shura 42:38)

In this verse, we are reminded that consultation is a type of conduct that is on the same level as prayer; we are reminded of the significance of consultation by the fact that the answer to and acceptance of God's word or invitation and its consequences, such as prayers, consultation and giving, are mentioned in the same divine commandment.

That is why a society which does not consider consultation important can hardly be considered to be a fully believing one, and a community which does not apply consultation is not accepted as being Muslim in the full and perfect sense. In Islam, consultation is an absolute essential, which both the rulers and the ruled must obey. The ruler is responsible for conducting consultation about political, governing, legislation and all affairs related to society; the ruled are responsible for expressing and conveying their views and thoughts to the ruler.

The important things which should be noted are: consultation is the first condition for the success of a decision made on any issue. We have all seen how all decisions made without having been thought through thoroughly, without having taken into account the views and criticisms of others, whether related to individuals in particular or to society in general, have resulted in fiasco, loss, and great disappointment. Even if a person has a superior nature and outstanding intellect, if they are content with their own opinions and are not receptive and respectful to the opinions of others, then they are more prone to make mistakes and errors than the average person. The most intelligent person is the one who most appreciates and respects mutual consultation and deliberation (*mashwarat*), and who benefits most from the ideas of others. Those who are content with their own ideas in their plans and deeds, or who even insist or force others to accept their ideas, not only miss a very important dynamic, but also face disagreement, hostility, and hatred from the people with whom they are associated.

Just as the first condition for one to obtain the best results in any task one undertakes is mutual consultation, equally it is by means only of mutual consultation that one is able to gain a significant source of power that is far superior to one's own.

Before any venture one should not spare any effort in carrying out the necessary preliminary investigation, deliberation, and consultation in order to avoid criticizing the destiny and blaming others associated with the doer and the work on the basis of causes, in order to stay within the plan of precautions, and in order not to thus delve further into harmful behavior and consequences which could lead to downfall or calamity. Disappointment and remorse are inevitable if the outcome and consequences have not been well thought-out and deliberated and if the people experienced in that field have not been referred to prior to the venture. Ventures and enterprises embarked on without sufficient prior consultation do not go far and also cause those who undertake them to lose credit and to become disheartened, discouraged, and disappointed.

Consultation is one of the prime dynamics which keep the Islamic order standing as a system. To consultation belongs the most important mission and duty of resolving affairs concerning the individual and the community, the people and the state, science and knowledge, and economics and sociology, unless of course there is a *nass* (divine decree; a verse of the Qur'an or a command from the Prophet, decisive on any point in canon law) with a clear meaning on these matters.

In Islam, the consultative council of the state is an institution in a position of guidance; it takes place prior to executive decisions. Today in some countries there is the supreme court, but its function is quite limited, its remit is quite narrow, and it is a much constrained institution compared to the Islamic consultation.

Even if the head of state or the leader is confirmed by God and nurtured by revelation and inspiration, he is under obligation to conduct affairs by consultation. There have been some who have neglected to do so, but generally the number of nations or communities which have retained this institution under different names and titles at different times is not negligible. In fact, any society which has ignored or disregarded it has never prospered, but rather has perished. So the Messenger of God saw the salvation and progress of his community in mutual consultation: "Those who consult can never lose."[6]

Consultation in the Qur'an is mentioned explicitly in two verses, but there are many more verses indicating it. The first of the two explicit verses were given above, and the second one, which does not require any interpretation whatsoever, is:

Consult them in the affairs (of moment). (Al 'Imran 3: 159)

It should also be noted that consultation is the key word in this chapter and how meaningful it is that the chapter is called Shura (Consultation), outlining one of the basic principles which characterize the community of true believers.

In this chapter, consultation is treated as a commendable attribute of the Companions. This is a reminder that has been phrased as if to say "Why should those [the Companions] whose every action is consultation-based not be praised?" That the Companions were praised particularly for consultation from among so many attributes can be considered a very important indicator of its significance.

Just as consultation is emphasized as an important rule in the Qur'an, we also witness that it has been given considerable weight in the Prophet's example (Sunna) and that its importance is underlined repeatedly. The Messenger of God always consulted others, whether men or women, young or old, on the matters on which a Divine Decree had not been revealed. Though we may be very advanced in various fields now, we cannot claim that we have today yet reached the level in consultation that had been reached at that time.

Consulting with his Companions on every matter, the Messenger of God took their opinions and perspectives into account, and thus every venture he planned was presented to and adopted by the collective conscience; he made use of every feeling, emotion, and inclination that arose from the collective conscience as a foundation, and thus he supported and gave extra strength and endurance to the work he undertook. That is, by uniting everyone and involving everyone mentally and spiritually in the work to be done, he accomplished his projects on the strongest, soundest basis.

Now we can relate some incidents from the life of the Prophet to illustrate this.

Before and after the Muslims arrived at Uhud, the Messenger of God took counsel with his Companions and instructed them to follow certain strategies during the battle. Among the strategies he employed, without having received any indirect or implied objections from the Companions were: to post the archers on a certain position on the hill; how the archers were to confront the enemies and take part in the battle; how they were not to change or leave their positions, no matter what should happen; that even if other soldiers should break ranks or run after the spoils after a clear victory, the archers were to hold their positions and continue to follow the command given and not to follow the other soldiers . . .

However, even though they realized the wisdom of obeying commands, some of the Companions fell into the error of interpretation or judgment of when the given command was no longer valid, and thus they had an indirectly oppositional attitude, similar to that of the indirect opposition the Messenger of God had faced on the way to Uhud.[7] Now had anyone else been faced with such consecutive opposition, and had that person suffered the loss and damage that was suffered at that time, he would certainly have rebuffed those people and their ideas, and would have said, "Go away and may God punish you as you've deserved." But the Messenger of God did not do that. Though he had been injured and his face was covered with blood as a result of the ruthless attacks of the enemies to which his Companions' actions had inadvertently exposed him, and in spite of being surrounded by the mutilated bodies of many of his Companions and close relatives, and at a time when some of his friends had worried and fought for their lives and fled toward Madina to save their lives, God's Messenger recited the verse, *Conduct the affairs by mutual consultation* to those around him, whether guilty or not, as if nothing had happened, and sat and consulted with them again about their next move. Not only did he take counsel with them, but at the same time he also informed them that they would be pardoned and he received the

Divine Revelation that commanded him to pray for their forgiveness:

> And by the mercy of God you dealt with them gently. And had
> you been severe and harsh-hearted, they would have been bro-
> ken away from about you; so pass over (their faults), and ask
> (God's) forgiveness for them; and consult them in the affairs.
> Then when you have taken a decision, put your trust in God,
> certainly God loves those who put trust in Him. (Al 'Imran
> 3:159)

When this verse was revealed following the Battle of Uhud,
God's Messenger is reported to have said: "Indeed neither God
nor His Messenger need consultation. However, God made it a
means for [His] Mercy. Whoever consults, he is not denied
attaining the right, and whoever leaves it falls into deviation." It
can be clearly understood by this statement that as God
enjoined consultation upon His Messenger, who did not need it,
then so too must other rulers or administrators practice it. The
rulers are reminded that they should not exercise dictatorship
and that they should benefit from the ideas of their citizens; this
is how citizens can provide assistance to the governing of the
state.

A few of the Prophet's remarks on consultation, taken from
many, are given below:

> One who consults will not have cause to regret.[8]
>
> One who consults will not come to harm.[9]
>
> One who consults is secure.[10]
>
> There has been no community which used consultation but
> could not reach the right result.[11]

Considering all these, there is consensus among Islamic
scholars that consultation is one of the basic principles of Islam
and that it is one of the necessary rules that should be applied to

life. It has always been understood and practiced so, although some differences in its application can be seen through different ages and times and under some special conditions and circumstances.

***

Clearly consultation does not take priority over Divine Commands as a source of legislation. It is itself enabled by Divine Commands, and though it may be the basis for some laws and principles, consultation is restricted as it depends on true legislative sources. Those matters on which there is a clear divine decree remain outside the intervention of human beings, and people may only turn to consultation in order to ascertain its full meaning. Matters on which there is no such a decree are considered completely within the boundaries of consultation. On such matters, there is an obligation to abide by the results and decisions reached by consultation, and one cannot act contrary to the decisions taken and cannot continue to expound or defend other opposing views and opinions. If there is an error or mistake in the decision taken, even if it was taken by the majority, it must be amended or corrected by consultation again.

Although the divine decrees about consultation are, in a sense, general, they are restricted by the decrees on particular issues and also by the acts and deeds of the Messenger of God. In fact the decrees in Islam, with a few exceptions (those which express universal principles and general rules), do not dwell much upon or go into details of matters which can be deemed secondary. Issues on which there is no decree fall completely within the boundaries of consultation and are of the matters open to deliberation.

Having accepted the fact that every matter on which Islam clearly ordains a decree is outside the limits of consultation and the matters on which Islam does not have a clear decree remain within the boundaries of consultation, consultation is then restricted by the rule that it abides by and accords with Islam under all conditions and circumstances, and that it must be regulated by reference to the Qur'an and Sunna and that it [*shura*] tries to realize the objectives described and defined by the Word of God, the Qur'an. The following are among the first principles at which Islam aims: to establish equality among people; to strive against ignorance and to spread knowledge; to interweave and interlace every issue and affair around the Islamic identity so that Muslims are not left to contradict their own essence; to direct the people of a country to protect their place and standing in the balance between states; to achieve the right balance of social justice between the individual and community; to develop and advance in every individual and the whole nation feelings of love, respect, altruism, striving for the sake of others, sacrificing their own material and spiritual benefits, and aspirations for the sake of others; to maintain and retain the balance between this world and the other; to order and organize domestic and international politics; to follow world affairs closely; and to prepare, as and when needed, all the resources to cope with the world as a whole, including the preparation and modernization of teams to counter psychological warfare. All these are human concerns, on which all the great rulers, administrators, gifted thinkers, and philosophers have always put great emphasis. Within the guidance of legislating and representation, the Prophet of Islam always strove for these goals, and based people's lives, cultural affairs, ventures, deeds and relationships with one another upon all these principles; in this way he was able to unite their feelings, thoughts, minds, logic, perceptions, and hearts.

***

Consultation, within its remit, promises some effects and also follows some rules which lead to positive outcomes. In this regard we may mention an increase in the level of thought and intervention in society; reminding society of its own importance by taking its views on all new events; by reminding it in this way, leading it to produce alternative ideas; keeping consultation as an active principle for the sake of the future of Islam; in every event, getting the *Sawaad al-A'zam* (the majority of the highest, most able individuals or the council of the Muslim community) to join in the administration to some extent; to ensure by public supervision of the administration that the people remain aware of the necessity for questioning and calling to account the administrators whenever the situation requires them to do so; and by preventing irresponsible behavior of rulers by limiting their executive power.

As we stated above, it is because of this vital importance of consultation that God commends the Companions of Prophet Muhammad as those *who conduct their affairs by mutual consultation* (Shura 42:38). Furthermore, the fact that toward the end of the battle of Uhud, at its most painful moment, God once more commands the Prophet to *consult, take counsel of them* (Al 'Imran, 3:159) with the Companions, who have caused such a bitter outcome and painful time, is exceptionally important.

Both of the revealed verses related to the principle of consultation are extremely flexible and responsive to the needs of every era; they have a breadth which surpasses all ages, such that, no matter how much the world changes and no matter how the times alter, even if humans were able to build cities in the sky, they would not feel the need to add new things to these decrees (the two verses). In fact, all the other rules and principles of Islam are open to similar flexibility and universality, and have always retained, and will also retain in the future, their freshness, relevance and validity, despite the passing of time.

It would be useful to recap the points of what forms the basis of consultation.

1. Consultation is a right for both the ruling and the ruled; and in exercising that right neither has preference, priority, or superiority over the other. In the verse *who conduct their affairs by mutual consultation* (Shura 42:38), the Qur'an indicates that both sides, the ruling and the ruled, have equal status: as all the work related to the Muslims concerns every individual and the whole community, the rights of the ruler and the ruled are accepted as being equal. However, the right may vary according to time, place, and conditions, and thus the way to conduct consultation may vary.

2. As a consequence of the verse, *consult them in the affairs* (Al 'Imran 3:159), it is incumbent on the ruler or administrator to bring the matter on which consultation is required to the attention of those of sound judgment, otherwise he will be held responsible. The ruled are responsible for expressing their views when they are asked to. However, if the ruled do not express their views when asked to, then they are equally accountable. In fact, they are considered not to have fulfilled the duty of citizenship if they are not determined to be heard when their views are being taken, and still more if they neglect to voice their views and opinions.

3. Performing consultation for the pleasure of God and the benefit of the Muslims, and not allowing the line of thought of the consultative committee to be affected or deflected by bribery, threats, or oppression are essential. God's Messenger said: "One who is consulted is a man of trust; one who is consulted about a matter must express his view as if he were deciding for himself."

4. There may not be always unanimity (*ijma'*) in consultation. However, in a case where there is no general concurrence or consensus of opinion and decisions amongst those present, the decision is taken and people act according to the opinion

and conviction of the majority. According to God's Messenger, the majority is considered to represent full agreement:

> God's hand is with the community.[12]
>
> My people do not unite around deviation.[13]
>
> I asked God not to let my people unite on deviation, and He accepted my wish.[14]

In these hadiths, we are reminded that the majority view is as powerful as unanimity and we must apply and abide by the decision of the majority. We can relate many examples of this from the Prophet's own life, and in short we can say that the consultations at the beginning and the end of the battles of Badr and Uhud were carried out in this way.

5. Whether concluded by unanimity or by the majority, as long as consultation is conducted by the rules, in conformity with the principles of consultation, it is then no longer permissible to disagree with or oppose the decisions taken, or to propose alternative ideas. To continue to air views against the decision taken with words such as "[but] I suggested a different and sounder view" or "[but] I already made a remark or comment in opposition" leads only to defeat, and is nothing less than a sin. God's Messenger went to Uhud in compliance with the view of the majority, though it was against his own judgment (*ijtihad*); after the battle, he did not say or make any remark concerning the view of the majority, its cause, and the aftermath, even though their view had been erroneous. Moreover, the Qur'an indicated that the *zalla* (lapse, slip) of the *muqarrabin* (the close ones) which was committed during the preparation for Uhud could be questioned.[15]

6. Consultation is concerned with resolving existing problems. It does not call for conjectural decisions related to hypothetical events. In any case, Islamic life is already continuing in the light of divine decrees. As to the events which occur outside

that frame or as to other plans and projects that must be fully realized, each and every plan or event, by taking its particularity into full account should be resolved by itself, within itself, and according to its own manner of taking place.

7. The consultative committee convenes when the need arises and continues to work until the problems have been resolved, and the plans and projects finalized. As there is no divine decree that it should convene at regular intervals, so is there no indication that it should be composed of salaried or paid individuals; the practice of the Prophet and the first four Caliphs constitute the parameters in this respect, we are not concerned with the practices of the following periods. As a matter of fact, the execution of consultation by salaried people or officials causes many problems and complications along with it.

***

We have to touch on the question of the people with whom we can consult. As it is impossible to bring all the people of a country together and to conduct a consultation in this way, then it must be done with a cadre of a limited number of people. Moreover, since the matters presented for deliberation require a great degree of knowledge, experience, and expertise, consultation committee must be comprised of people who are distinguished for such qualities. This can only be a committee of people of high caliber, who are able to resolve many matters.[16] Especially today, as life has become more intricate and complicated, as the world has globalized, and every problem has become an all-encompassing, planetary problem, it is vital that those competent in natural sciences, engineering, and technology, which are most of the time considered to be good and proper by Muslims, should participate alongside those men of high caliber who know Islamic essence, reality, spirit, and sciences. Consultation can be carried out with qualified people from the different worldly sciences, knowledge, and other required fields, insofar as decisions taken are supervised by the religious authorities for the compatibility or accord of what they suggest with Islam. As consultation is in itself left to this committee, the prescription of the way of performing it in accordance with different times, circumstances, and states of affairs also falls within their scope. Throughout history, it is possible to see differences in the performance and application of consultation corresponding to the different eras and particular circumstances. Sometimes in small circles or among small groups, and sometimes in wide circles or among larger groups, sometimes among civilians, and sometimes by opening its gates to the sciences and the military, the understanding of consultation itself has exhibited quite considerable change and differences. However, this is not because it is a rule subject to being changed, but because of its flexibility and the universality of its practicability in every age and era.

According to different circumstances and eras, the conduct and the composition of the consultative committee might change, but the qualifications and the attributes of those select people, such as people from knowledge, justice, social education and experience, wisdom, and sagacity, must never change. *Justice* means fulfilling all compulsory duties, but avoiding all that are forbidden and nothing contrary to human values should be done; *knowledge* comprises religious, administrative, political, and scientific expertise. Each individual does not have to be an expert in all the various branches of the sciences. However, the committee and the collective mind should be receptive to all the above-mentioned expertise. When good manners, experience, and social education lie at the root of the matter, the views and perspectives of experienced people are taken, even if they are not from the scientific community. *Wisdom* is knowledge, mildness, in a way, the essence of the Prophethood, and cognizance of what is behind the veiled reality of natural phenomena. It is seen as the knowledge which allows people to perceive with the light of sagacity and intuition and to understand what is closed to the common man, giving them the talents, abilities, and intelligence to resolve individual and social or collective problems. Wisdom is recognized as an attribute which is of very high value, but which is possessed by very few.

***

The importance the Messenger of God attached to consultation and his respect for the opinions of the old, the young, and people of different social ranks requires a full and separate treatment. However, within the scope of this article we will touch upon a few examples. He always consulted and listened to the views of others, took them seriously, and tried to establish all the alternative plans and projects on firm grounds. He proved how highly he regarded consultation by sometimes revealing his opinion one by one to individuals with sound opinion and judgment, and sometimes by bringing all those people together, and then basing the decision on a collective view:

1. On the occasion of the slander against his wife Aisha (*ifq*) the Messenger of God consulted several of his Companions, namely 'Ali, 'Umar, Zaynab bint-i Jahsh, and Barira. 'Ali expressed the opinion that God's Messenger should ignore his worries and disregard the baseless slanders; 'Umar, Zaynab, Barira and many highly esteemed others stated that they believed Aisha to be chaste, exalted, and purified of such calumnies. Although the chain of narrators is not considered strong, a conversation is reported between 'Umar and God's Messenger when he asked 'Umar's opinion about the event. 'Umar said: "One day, while you were leading the congregational prayer, you took off your slippers and pushed them aside. When we asked the reason for it, you replied that something

impure had smudged your slippers and the Archangel Gabriel
came and informed you of it and asked you to take off your slippers. Now, if something had happened and blemished the good
·name of your wife, would God not have informed you of it?'
Even though the authenticity of this conversation is not held to
be high by some scholars of hadith, the lesson from it in respect
of taking counsel is quite important.

2. Before setting out for the Battle of Badr, God's
Messenger consulted the Muhajirun and Ansar.[17] Miqdad, on
behalf of the Muhajirun and Sa'd ibn Muadh on behalf of the
Ansar expressed similar views overflowing with faith, submission, and enthusiasm, which agreed with, confirmed, and supported the view of God's Messenger, thus serving to convince
their tribes and the community present there that they should
fulfill the decisions taken. As can be seen from that occasion, the
Prophet always had such vital decisions taken and adopted by
the community as a whole, and proceeded toward the target by
having the public opinion along with him.

3. Again in preparation for the Battle of Badr, the
Messenger of God took the counsel of Companions such as
Khubab ibn Munzir about the positions and the fields of battle
where the army of Islam would be deployed, and decided on
and used strategies in line with these suggestions. The Muslims
then defeated an army three times ·as great as their own and
returned to Madina singing songs of victory.

4. During the Battle of Trench (Ahzab), his willingness to
heed and comply with the suggestion of Salman al-Farisi that
the Muslims should dig ditches around the spots where the
enemy was likely to try to infiltrate Madina is another example
of how God's Messenger attached importance to consultation.

5. During the negotiation of the Peace Treaty of Hudaybiya,
God's Messenger again consulted his Companions. After taking

the views of all the Muslims, he consulted with his wife, our mother, Umm Salama, not neglecting or ignoring her opinions, assessed the views and the personal inclinations of the Companions, then decided on a way and strategy which turned potentially complete defeat, complete failure, into a clear victory, and came back to Madina having saved the lives and souls of many.

When we look into the life of God's Messenger closely, we see that every matter, affair, or problem on which a Divine Revelation was not sent was conducted by consultation, presented to and adopted by the collective conscience, and then the decision was put into practice or executed. Thus the councils of consultation that we see in the various Islamic states throughout history are nothing more or less than a simple continuation of the first consultation and the council that we see in the Prophet's model.

ACTION AND THOUGHT

The field of our struggle for the inheritors of the Earth can be summarized as "action and thought." In fact, the true path of existence in life goes through a potentially transforming action and thought, which, is also able to transform others. In fact every existence, from this perspective, is the product of an action and some disciplines, and its continuance also depends on that action and those disciplines.

Action is the most important and necessary component of our lives. By undertaking particular responsibilities through continuous action and thinking, by facing and bearing particular difficulties, almost in a sense, by sentencing ourselves to all these, even though it may be at the expense of many things, we always have to act, to strive. If we do not act as we are, we are dragged into the waves caused by the thrust and actions of others, and into the whirlpools of the plans and thoughts of others, and then we are forced to act on behalf of others.

Remaining aloof from action, not interfering in the things happening around us, nor being a part of the events around us and staying indifferent to them, is like letting ourselves melt away, like ice turning into water. Such a melting away, which does not preserve our own molecules and molecular shape, is surrender and submission to events and occurrences which are contrary to our selves and our essence. Those who desire to remain true to themselves should really seek their essence with all their wishes, desires, hearts, conscience, behavior, deeds, and thoughts. For, in order to exist, the whole essence of the human being should be alert. Existence and its maintenance demand from humans the action of our arms, limbs, heart, and head. If we do not now devote our hearts and heads to our future existence, others may demand them insolently in a place and at a time which does not yield any benefit to us.

Being ourselves, uniting our wishes and desires with the wishes and desires of others, and then finding a course or direction of action for ourselves within existence as a whole, flowing as ourselves within our own course within the general currents and movements in the universe, preserving our own line while being integrated with the whole of existence are the most obvious aspects of Islamic action and thought. As regards one's own world, a person who is unable to connect with or relate to the whole of existence and does not perceive a connection or relation with the universe is attached to and bound by their individual and trivial wishes and wants, they who are closed to general and universal truths are those who cleave, alienate, and exclude themselves from existence as a whole and condemn and cast themselves into the death cell of egoism. All the carnal desires and ambitions, all the struggles around the material and corporeal and all the empty and self-delusive consolations which are sought in carnal desires, the corporeal and the material, arise undoubtedly from the complete detachment from true existence of a person and thus being left all alone. The real world of the person of action and thought and their real happiness in it are colored with the tones of universality and engraved within the frame of eternity. In this way, their world appears as one without beginning and without end; and should it have any beginning or end, it exceeds our conception and imagination. From this aspect, when we talk of a "happy person," we have in mind this sort of person. It is indeed impossible to call happiness which has a beginning and an end true happiness.

Seen from another, better angle, action is the embracing of the whole of existence with the most sincere and heartfelt decisions, the analysis of existence and the journeying toward eternity through the corridors of creation, and then by using the full power of the intellect and willpower, by means of the secrets and strength gained from the Infinite, placing one's own world into its true orbit and course that was preordained in its creation, disposition, and natural constitution.

As for thought, it is an inner action. Systematic and purposeful thought is enquiring the universe we are faced with for all the secrets and enigmas in its process of creation, and finding and exploring these answers. In other words, thought is the activity of a truth-seeking consciousness by establishing a kinship between the whole of existence and humanity everywhere and in the language peculiar to each thing.

It is by means of thought that the human spirit becomes intimate, inextricably interlaced, and intertwined with the universe, and thus continuously acquires greater and greater depths in itself; by breaking into pieces the narrow patterns of calculating reason or everyday understanding, it overflows and saves itself from the conjectures, delusions, and narrow confines of the mind, thus awakening to the realities, the absolute truths, which never mislead. In other words, thought is the emptying of the inner being to prepare room for metaphysical experiences in the depths of the inner being. If this is the first step of thinking, then the last step is active thinking.

The underlying dynamic of our life of action and thought is our spiritual life; it is not possible for us to separate our spiritual life from our religious thoughts. Our struggle for existence was carried out by relying on the Islamic spirit and essence. Just as any seed sprouts when it is dropped into the soil and any bud blossoms when it is exposed to sunlight, so too did we come to be with the profundities and qualities in our essence when we turned to and embraced Islam. This turning to and reaching for our essence caused the skills and the potential in our nature to develop, and secured our existence and continuance for centuries. Again, just as our partaking of the level of heart and soul within the inner world was achieved by worship, remembrance, and thinking, so embracing the whole creation, feeling Him in our pulse, and sensing Him in all the faculties of the mind are again dependent on the consciousness of worship and our endeavor in reflection and remembrance. Indeed, every act of a true believer is an act of worship; their every thought is an act of self-discipline, of self-control, of self-supervision; their every speech is a prayer, supplication, and episode of spiritual knowledge; their every observation of existence is a close study and investigation; and their relationships with others are divine compassion. To reach such a degree of spirituality or saintliness is dependent on being open to perception, logic, and reasoning, and thence to thoughts and inspiration from the Divine. In other words, it is very difficult for a person to reach this peak, to acquire such a state, unless experience has been sieved by the filter of the reason, reason has surrendered to the greatest intellect and foresight of the prophets, logic has turned completely into love, and love has evolved into love of God. If these have been accomplished, then as a result science turns out to be a dimension of religion and becomes religion's servant; intellect turns out to be a ray of light which reaches everywhere with the hand of inspiration; knowledge gained through experience turns out to be a prism reflecting the spirit of existence; and everything resounds with the song of spiritual knowledge, love and affection, and spiritual joy.

Although certain sections of our society share the same feelings and thoughts, and the same or almost the same spiritual mood, despite so much common ground, they are unable to act as positively as may be expected. If they sometimes err, go astray and fall repeatedly into opposition, the reasons for their conduct should be sought in the fact that that they are not or have not been able to become believers in the true sense. For no matter what conditions, pressures, or negative influences a true believer may be prone or subjected to, their behavior must always be colored in faith and their actions well-considered and thoughtful.

Therefore, the inheritors of the Earth who plan to build the world of the future should be aware of what kind of world they would like to build and of what kind of jewels they should use in its construction, so that they will not feel obliged to later destroy with their own hands what they have built with the same hands. Our essentials and spiritual roots are certain and obvious. The architects of the light of the future, by using their power of thought along with their dynamism of action, by benefiting fully from the flexibility, vastness, and universality of the historical dynamics, on which they will base our religious and national life, and of course by preserving observance of the Qur'an, Sunna and the authentic judgments derived from the Qur'an and Sunna by the early Islamic scholars, will once more try to receive the voice of Islam, to catch its line of thought, to read its pulse, and to listen to its heart, according to the comprehension, manner, and understanding of the age; lest they experience the inactivity of the intermediary world after death (*barzakh*) on the way to resurrection. This, first of all, depends on distancing oneself from all the drives and pressures of the carnal, and on being open to and sailing forth to spirituality, and on knowing and accepting this world as the waiting room for the beyond. In other words, this could be realized by enhancing the quantity of our religious practice and worship with quality; remedying that deficiency which is due to the mere mechanical counting of devotions in our remembrance and recitations with the depth and sincerity of our intention; and praying and supplicating with the awareness, caution, and reverence of addressing and petitioning the Being Who is closer to us than we are to ourselves. These are all understood and accomplished by those who pray and experience prayer as if they were walking toward the *Mi'raj*[18]; by those who experience fasting as if they were withdrawing into seclusion in Divine secrets; by those who give alms with the attitude of a trustee relieved of his charge, saying "Oh, I am relieved, freed from the burden of safeguarding these"; and by those who experience the pilgrimage as attendance at an international congress at which the issues and problems related to the Islamic world will be discussed, in a place where both the heart and soul can observe the luminosity, splendor, awe, and majesty of the beyond, of the higher realms of existence.

The sighting and achievement of all the above-mentioned noble aims depend on there being spiritual physicians who can diagnose and treat our inner and outer ailments and on there being guides who are always in constant contact with the beyond and never mislead; guides whose world of thought stretches from the material to the immaterial, from physics to metaphysics, from philosophy to Sufism. Such people were, and have always been, behind all the periods of prosperity in the past, and such will also represent the next movements of reconstruction and revival. This representation will be achieved by developing new judicial doctrines, based on the Qur'an and the Sunna, in the light of the latest events, developments, and future happenings; by adorning their own views with the new   perspectives and understandings of world affairs; by clarifying and improving their national spirit and consciousness with the perspective of Islam; by developing the freshest interpretations of art, attached to the sense of contemplative abstraction and congruous with the universality of Islam; and by re-molding our own culture, which combines the world and religion, and which has survived and endured for some thousand years.

Such representation, with this range, will advance our life of science, knowledge, philosophy, art, and religion ahead of other nations of the world in the coming years, it will direct all aspects of life and will make all our children, whether they have received schooling or not, and who are idle, aimless, and on the street, turn into people of ideas, skill, knowledge, and craftsmanship. As a result, all the streets will have the air of schoolrooms, the prisons will turn into centers of education and enlightenment, and homes will be transformed into corners of Paradise and emit the air of Paradise. The sciences and knowledge will walk hand in hand with religion everywhere; belief and reason, intertwined in close embrace, will yield and spread their fruit everywhere; the future, within the bosom of hope, aspiration, and resolution, will sprout and flourish, more colorfully, elegantly, and richly than in the utopias; all the media—radio, television, newspapers, journals—will shower enlightenment, abundance, and light all around; and every heart, except the fossilized, will walk around tasting and enjoying *kawthar*[19] in this heavenly spring.

This new genesis will be born of our own historical values, civilizations, culture, and romanticism. It will arise, on the one hand, from the mood and state of suffering, ill-treatment, injustice, condemnation, and oppression we have endured over the ages, and on the other, from the enthusiasms of our hearts, which are satisfied, saturated with faith, and which are always spiritually alert and ready to exert themselves.

To fulfill such a vital mission depends firstly on the power which will move the decayed spirits in this decayed ground. The levers pushed up and down over the last fifty years to set this process in motion seem to have begun to shift. In the words of the Turkish poet M. Akif Ersoy, we can say, "Strike with your pickaxe. Most is gone, little is left." The first action is the action of the soul, and it is now like the softness of serenity (*sakina*[20]); like the warmth and gentleness of a promising spring cloud, and like the arc of a rainbow over our heads, it greets us wherever we go. We believe it will not be long before that action of the soul will embrace warmly the land of the oppressed, ill-treated, and wrongly-condemned, and shower its mercy, compassion, and blessings on them.

Today might, to a large extent, has almost completely dissolved into the pattern of truth, and has surrendered to it. Of course, there is reason or justification for the existence of might, and many matters are almost impossible to resolve without it. Yet there is no doubt that might which deviates from truth and even opposes it is harmful; we can accept might which unites and coheres with truth as being the truth. Courage which arises from the integration of might with truth is not unjust, cruel, or tyrannical, but rather is the protector of the oppressed, the wronged, and the ill-treated, and it is the tongue which speaks for truth. What is important after this is its representation by the people of action and thought. In the following section, we shall present some of our people of action.

THE HERO OF THOUGHT AND ACTION

The person of thought and action moves actively while making plans; they are deeply concerned with bringing peace to the world, and representing the movement of raising once again the statues of our soul and meaning, which we have been knocking down continuously for centuries; and they render our historical values into our day. They are able to shift efficiently between action and thought with their will and reason, and are a people of activity who weave for us the newest of lace in full harmony with the canvas of our own soul and meaning.

They have always been inspired by "peace" along their journey, from feelings to thoughts, and from there on to every phase of practical life. Their unique objective is to construct and build up. They are the spiritual soldiers of the Truth who, instead of conquering countries and winning victory after victory, utilizing their material force and power, train the "general staff" of the soul, the architects of thought, and the workers of new ideas; they always beam out thoughts about construction and lead their disciples to restore the ruins; they are the spiritual soldiers enthused with zeal and thankfulness who have been able to unite their will with the Infinite Will, transform their poverty into prosperity, and their weakness into strength. As long as they can make use of these sources of power in accord with and loyal to the Owner, they can never be beaten; or in cases where it is wrongfully assumed that they have been beaten, they will appear at the head of another victorious stronghold.

The person of thought and action might assume different roles in society: sometimes a loyal patriot, a hero of thoughtful action, sometimes a devoted disciple of science and learning, an artist of genius, a statesperson, and sometimes all of these. Recent history has recorded a considerable number of people who have exemplified roles like these. Some of them lived with their thoughts out ahead of their actions, whereas others had both on the same level. Yet again there are people of action whose thoughts were completely concealed and unseen.

Ahmed Hilmi of Plovdiv, Mustafa Sabri Bey, Ferit Kam, Muhammed Hamdi Yazır, Süleyman Efendi, Ahmed Naim, Mehmed Akif, Necip Fazıl and Bediüzzaman are just a few names that we can mention among those many distinguished characters. To be able to keep within the boundaries of this short text, I am not going to delve into biographical details, but will just try to shed a little light upon their life stories.

Ahmed Hilmi of Filibe (Plovdiv) (1865-1914)

Born in Plovdiv, Bulgaria, the son of the Turkish ambassador, he started his education at Galatasaray Lycee (Mekteb-i Sultani) and got to know about the era there; he then moved to Izmir, after which he was posted to Beirut. In the meantime, he was in contact with the Young Turks, and as a result was exiled to Fizan; he later returned to Istanbul following the establishment of the Constitutional government, flagshipping the thought of *Ittihad-i Islam* (the Union of Islam) and publishing a journal under the same name, standing as the spokesperson of this school. Later, he started working for another daily paper, *Hikmet*, which was a platform for his confrontation with Ittihad ve Terakki Cemiyeti (Committee of Union and Progress) he went on to work on many other journals and magazines, taught philosophy for a while at Darulfunun (Istanbul University).

Ahmed Hilmi finally died at a very young age, poisoned by Freemasons, who were his archenemies.

This very distinguished man of thought and action, on whom we are casting a passing glance, a person who left behind so many works, is waiting in the pages of history to be discovered.

Ferit Kam (1864-1944)

The life journey of this notable person of thought, delicate taste, and master of language, who was active at a very young age in the cultural life of Istanbul, is as follows: he was a teacher of French and had an interest in philosophy. After pursuing this interest for a while he fell into a temporary depression, but subsequently, by Divine Grace, found shelter in Sufism and once again was able to find a balance; he wrote for the journals *Sirat-ı Müstakim* and *Sebilürreşad*; he taught as a professor at Darulfunun and Süleymaniye Madrasa; he joined Daru'l-Hikmeti'l Islamiye (Council of Islamic Wisdom), enduring dismissals and re-designations to his position and never-ending suffering and deprivations. The end result was that, like every other hero of thought and action, he led a very colorful life dedicated to the Hereafter, until the day he walked to God.

Volumes of books would not suffice to describe his entire exalted life. Based upon critiques and commentaries, this intellectual of the twentieth century should most certainly be found on the curriculum of today's generations; he is a rich source of inspiration.

Mustafa Sabri Bey (1869-1954)

This genuine child of Anatolia was a hero of struggle; he worked as a professor, an officer of the palace library, a deputy in Parliament, the chief writer of *Beyanu'l Hak*, was a member of the Hürriyet ve Itilaf Fırkası (Independence and Union Party) and finally was appointed to the *sheikhulislam*; he always appeared as a hero of action and struggle until he was forced to leave the country after the Babıali Raid[21]; aggravating circumstances compelled him to continue his services in a different Muslim country, but he returned, as he had sought opportunities to continue his cause in Turkey; he became a member of the *Daru'l Hikmeti'l Islamiye*, and later was assigned as the *sheikhulislam*, which was his last opportunity to serve his country. In 1922 he left Turkey for Romania, then Iskece (Greece), and later died in Egypt in 1954, having completed a life full of ceaseless strife, an anguished life, with highs and lows, but more than rich enough to provide research for many dissertations.

Babanzade Ahmed Naim (1872 - 1934)

Born in Baghdad, Ahmed Naim was the son of a pasha. Like his peers, his educational life was nourished in Istanbul. This outstanding character was endowed with a vast world of thinking and feelings; he studied at Galatasaray Lycee, Mülkiye School (School for Civil Service), became an officer at the Translation Department of the Ministry of Foreign Affairs, and then the director of Instruction in the Ministry of Education. He later became a member of the Translation Office, taught at the Faculty of Literature, Darulfunun, and was finally appointed rector for a while.

Leaving an enormous scientific and educational legacy to the next generations, Ahmet Naim is an important source who has nourished present-day Turkish society, philosophically as well as spiritually.

Mehmed Akif Ersoy (1873 - 1936)

Volumes of books have already been written about this sincere patriot; he is beyond description. Many commentaries and critiques have been composed about him and I believe many others will voice his faith, love, enthusiasm, activism, cause, and thoughts. He is one of the very few Turkish intellectuals of his time who travelled Anatolia, Rumeli (European Turkey), and Arabia. At every town where he stopped, he pronounced the sorrowful longing of a very noble but unfortunate nation and his poetic sighs made others shudder. He managed to maintain his path as a sincere and dedicated public figure all through his lifetime, starting as a veterinary surgeon, and later becoming an official inspector, to teaching literature at Darulfunun, and as a member of *Sırat-ı Müstakim*, participating in Daru'l-Hikmeti'l-Islamiye, and delivering numerous sermons during the Turkish National War.[22]

We are grateful for the research that has already been carried out on the life and works of Mehmed Akif. We continue to look forward to a future where more serious attention is paid to research on the many past activists of thought and art, like this son of Turkish nation, who lived in piety like the Companions of the Prophet and walked to the Hereafter completely destitute of any worldly possessions.

Elmalılı Muhammed Hamdi Yazır (1878 - 1942)

He was a scholar of stature widely respected throughout the world. After attending primary school in Elmalı, a small town in Anatolia, he moved on to the capital to complete his education. He took lessons from very distinguished scholars, acquired his diploma in theology, taught and lectured at Mekteb-i Nuvvab and Medresetu'l Vaizin. He later became a Member of Parliament in the Second Constitutional Government. Due to an incorrect interpretation on his part, he signed the juridical decision (*fatwa*) for the dethronement of Sultan Abdulhamid II; he was a member of Darul-Hikmeti'l-Islamiye and Minister of Charities. After being prosecuted by the "independence courts," he was saved from execution, and he went into a very long-lasting seclusion, during which his marvelous Qur'anic commentary was written. Hamdi Yazır holds a very special place in our history of philosophy and activism.

Necip Fazıl Kısakürek (1905 - 1983)

The ancestors of Necip Fazıl came from Maraş, but he himself was born in Istanbul and grew up as an Istanbul gentleman. The American College and Naval School were the two places that played a significant role in his early life, providing him with an environment that enabled him to discover his talents. After studying philosophy at Darulfunun, he departed for the Sorbonne, where he met with the West for the first time. After working as a bank inspector, he unwillingly ventured into business for a short time. He provided artistic inspiration for everyone with or without talent at the State Conservatoire and at the Academy of Fine Arts. He was the designer, architect, and suffering owner of the *Büyük Doğu* (Great East) school of thought, as well as publishing a journal of the same name. This journal was closed down many times, but continued to go on publishing again and again, each time with a new program devised during the closure, driven by the prodigious will behind it. Necip Fazıl was a master of poetry and prose, as well as a worker of ideas for the future. His vast Sufi way of thinking, metaphysical wisdom, life-long respect for the Absolute Truth, veneration and self-assurance for the spirit of the Prophet, the Master of all existence, are but a few of the drops from the vast oceans of his admirable qualities which he demonstrated in various fields. This great man deserves to be analyzed in all his aspects and to be introduced to Turkish youth, indeed to the entire world, through the establishment of an institute carrying his name.

Süleyman Efendi (Hilmi Tunahan 1888 - 1959)

Child of a noble family in Silistre, Süleyman Efendi returned to and started teaching in his hometown, like his father. Having reached a high level of maturity, he was able to combine his spiritual wealth with the education he had received in Istanbul. His family, anticipating his mission and bright future, were thankful that what they had expected had come true, and were overjoyed as they saw the expanding circle of students, companions, and brothers gathering around him in utter submission and loyalty.

Süleyman Efendi was a hero of struggle, one of those very rare people who never show any weariness throughout their life. He determinedly defended the Sunni way of belief, as he chose to struggle at a time when religious feelings and thinking were constantly under attack. He weaved the lacework of our soul, using religious thought and historical consciousness as a canvas; he tried to make the essentials of existence audible to all by opening schools, hostels, and boarding houses all around the country, and he never retreated from carrying out his mission until the day of his death.

It is impossible to describe this great man of action in a few lines. To describe such a hero of soul and meaning would take up many volumes of books. This hero, despite many obstructions, furnished every corner of the country, from Edirne to Ardahan, with education and learning in a very short time.

We shall leave the analysis of the mission, action, interpretation, and philosophy of this very important personality to the research of academics with enquiring and spiritually open minds, hoping that this small attempt may later be transformed into much greater works.

* * *

When considering the intellectuals of the second half of the twentieth century, we have to bear in mind Nureddin Topçu, a real son of the nation, a creative thinker, a hero of love and excitement—despite some of his controversial approaches which conflict with our basic criteria. We must take note of Sezai

Karakoç, the very distinguished intellectual and great thinker, the great poet and author of the century, who patiently incubated thought for the future, persevering on his path with the utmost pains, but in silence. We must recall with the greatest respect Es'ad Efendi, Sami Efendi, Arvasi Hazretleri, Ali Haydar Efendi, Mehmed Zahit Kotku, Imam of Alvar, Seydah of Serdehl, and Muhammed Raşit Efendi of Menzil and think about their love, enthusiasm and actions in the tradition of serving others.

And could it ever be possible to ignore Bediüzzaman, who overturned all the plans of unbelievers and atheists with his strong faith, thoughts, and head-spinning activism?

So much has been said and written all over the world about this writer, one of the most widely read authors of the century, a man whose works have been translated into all the major languages. Long descriptions are not required to make him better known, so it will suffice to quote a short passage from the introduction written for one his works.

Bediüzzaman Said Nursi (1877 - 1960)

Bediüzzaman's life is a rich source of research for scholars, enabling them to present his work and personality to all of humanity. He was the number one figure of the modern age who succeeded in presenting Islam's vast ocean of faith, moral values, and conscience in the most efficient and purest way. A sentimental attachment to Bediüzzaman and his thoughts is not an adequate way of remembering him and his works. Sentimentalism does not sit well with the seriousness of the issues he persistently examined and bravely proclaimed. He led his life in the shade of the Book and the Prophet's tradition, and under the wings of experience and logic, a man of sound judgment filled with love and enthusiasm to an incomparable degree.

Many publications and conferences have been dedicated to Bediüzzaman's outstanding qualities such as devotion to lofty ideals and his deep concern for today's world, simplicity, all-embracing humanism, loyalty, fidelity to his friends, chastity, humility, modesty, and contentedness. As a matter of fact, each of these qualities deserves to be studied in separate volumes, and Bediüzzaman frequently refers to them in his works. Moreover, there are so many of his companions still among us, each of whom is a living witness blessed with the good fortune of having been close to him during his lifetime and having seen in person his spiritual vastness and intellectual prosperity.

His outward appearance was quite plain and simple for such a scholar. However, he always displayed a very strong character through his thoughts and life of activism, seen in few other historical personalities. He embraced the whole of humanity with regard to the universal matters that all people suffer. He hated unbelief, tyranny, and apostasy, and fought against despotism smiling in the face of death. He displayed loyalty to his cause and chivalry to such a degree that he felt nothing but contempt for his own survival. Besides being highly spiritual in his personal life in the matters concerning his mission, he always managed to act in accordance with the Qur'an and the Sunna, and in the guidance of reasoning and logic. His behavior was shaped by the two parts of his pure inner character: the first was a heroic person, a great soldier of conscience, a man of love and enthusiasm; the second was a far-sighted thinker, leading his contemporaries from the fore, a balanced intellectual putting forward outstanding plans and projects. This perspective on Bediüzzaman is highly significant, as one of the rings in the chain of great people in Islamic history, will help us comprehend better what he really means for us in this age.

Although some seem purposefully to ignore him, his contemporaries acknowledged Bediüzzaman to be the most serious thinker and writer of his time, the spokesperson and leader of the masses, while still managing to maintain his humility and keep himself away from any kind of ostentation. "Fame is the same as hypocrisy and a venomous honey which kills the heart," is one of his epithets on this topic. He has always been one of the most admired authors in the Islamic world of the twentieth century, and today is one admired all around the world. His works have been read carefully with sincere feelings of appreciation and will continue to be relevant as time passes.

Bediüzzaman's works are the fruit of a serious effort expounding on certain isssues needed to be addressed from the perspective of the time he was born into. The reader can hear the cries, hopes, and eagerness of Anatolia, as well as that of the entire Islamic world. Although he was born in a small village in one of the farthest corners of Eastern Anatolia, he expressed our feelings like a gentleman brought up in Istanbul and embraced the entire country with a vast compassion and pure sincerity.

Bediüzzaman directed our people, who were socially impaired by shocks one after another, to the fountain of Khidr,[23] and inspired resurrection with his works that glowed with faith and hope at a time when materialism had capsized our intellectual life, when communism had reached its climax, and the world was undergoing an unfortunate period filled with chaos. Before anyone else, he confronted and tried to deal with the anarchy that was based on unbelief and atheism, defining it as a most significant problem that should be solved urgently. His efforts were outstanding and almost superhuman in this respect. Coming face to face with such a chaotic world, Bediüzzaman was fully conscious of the responsibility he had to shoulder, and as he bore this tremendous burden, he was a person of utmost modesty, while still having the full confidence one should have in God the All-Mighty's infinite power and never-ending bounty.

At a time when all of humanity was being dragged into atheism through the abuse of science and philosophy, when brains were being washed with communism, and those who were trying to stop these unfavorable developments were being sent into exile, when the most embarrassing deportations were being conducted in every corner of the country (and all of these were being done for the sake of civilization and modernization!), and when nihilism was the most widespread sorcery, Bediüzzaman reminded us of our inner jails, our various self-imprisonments in our souls, the murders and exiles that we commit against ourselves; he awakened human virtues in our spiritual dimension and conscience that had long been inactive; he quenched the thirst of our hearts with sublime knowledge; he displayed our inner capacities for the otherworld and poured down upon us all the wealth of our schools and Sufi lodges (*takka, zaviya, maktab, madrasa*).

At a wicked time when the nation was suffering from barren intellectualism, when every social problem developed into chaos, when people had to confront hundreds of blood-chilling events all over the country, and when Islamic and national values had been destroyed, Bediüzzaman analyzed the causes and proposed solutions like a prudent physician. He observed unfortunate generations sinking deeper into swamps of unbelief, deviation, and doubts as they strived to break out, and he felt deep in his conscience the gravity of the grim picture before him. his life was nevertheless filled with enthusiasm; he reflected continually, producing alternative ideas and presenting them to the government and society. He fought to remind this glorious but unfortunate nation and country of its vast legacy from the past.

Bediüzzaman traveled through many provinces of the country, starting at a time when *Devlet-i Aliye* (Ottomans) was still standing, and visited all the residential areas, from the largest cities to the remotest towns, the most populous areas, as well as almost deserted villages. He was appalled to see that in every place he stopped ignorance prevailed; the masses were suffering the abject poverty, and our people were impeding and damaging each other due to a variety of conflicts As a leading intellectual who interpreted his time at the highest level of understanding, he desired to inspire the desperate and miserable masses with a spirit of learning and knowledge. He pointed out the causes of the current poverty and economic problems, sought solutions for dissensions within the society, and continuously proclaimed unity and collective existence, never abandoning the nation to its destiny, even at the most chaotic times: "If all these intermingled troubles are not dealt with and our wounds are not treated by competent and specialized hands, our diseases will become chronic, and the wounds will become gangrenous. It is clear that we must identify our problems in relation to our learning, social existence, and administration; we must make a start on solving our troubles, whether materialistic or spiritual. This is how we can protect ourselves from more dangers to come, those that gnaw at our existence, shaking our foundations, and dragging us into deadly pits."

Bediüzzaman analyzed three major factors which were at the basis of all the troubles then, and still remain so today: ignorance, poverty, and social disunity. Ignorance, in the sense of indifference toward God and the Prophet, a lack of interest in religion and historical dynamics, is the primary trouble from which we suffer. Bediüzzaman dedicated his life to fighting this fatal virus. In his view, the hope of salvation for our nation would be in vain unless false and deviated ideologies were prevented, society was illuminated with learning, knowledge, and systematic thinking. It is due to this ignorance that the Qur'an and the universe have been separated from one another; the former became an orphan in the fantasy dungeons of fanatic souls, who are uninformed of the secrets of existence, formations, and phenomena, while the latter is perceived as nothing but chaos in the eyes of incomparably ignorant materialists who are totally blind to the spiritual realm.

Ignorance stands as the foremost reason today why this blessed part of the world is so afflicted with destitution and poverty, even when the same land is covered by the most productive plains, fields, and with flowing rivers; despite all this, the inhabitants today are little more than beggars waiting at the door.

Likewise, it is also a very interesting contrast that we are rundown, almost bent double under heavy foreign debts, even when we possess rich mines hidden underground; countless supplies obtained from our lands are being shoveled into the treasuries of others.

Due to ignorance and poverty again, laborers and farmers toil day and night, worn out by ceaseless work, with no full return for their efforts, gaining no wage that can lead them to affluence. They can never be happy, and one can see them deteriorate day by day, step by step.

Ignorance and the social unity it brings about prevent societies from taking action against disaster, exile, oppression, humiliation, misery, various addictions and the calamities that is endured in our lands, despite never-ending bloodshed, rape, and countless violations of human rights; the entire world is drifting unconsciously from one side to another, entrapped in the web of imbalance. In the face of all these, we fail to rid ourselves from disunity, unable to bring an end to this catastrophy and distress. We cannot provide the Islamic world with any remedy for its ailments; there is no cure for falling off yet another cliff, each cliff more dreadful with every passing day. We cannot be inspired with the spirit of unity, thus challenging the time in which we live.

We have been engulfed in pain due to the above mentioned circumstances; in the meantime, some among us have been overwhelmed, their eyes dazzled, their sight blurred, and their heads made dizzy by the ostensible and material progress of the West. Instead of attaining material-spiritual richness by engaging their minds with positive sciences and their hearts with religious truths, these enchanted people chose to behave as if they were totally without a soul and detached from their roots; they overlooked our most fatal national and religious dynamics, and deprived the masses of their morals, of their virtue, of their historical consciousness, isolating them from their own national character by blind imitation. Although this was meant to save society, blind imitation proved to be more harmful and induced incurable damage in the society's spirit.

Our society has suffered from this choking nightmare of ignorance and disunity for years, while also being separated from our national identity, devastating our virtues, spiritual nobility, and global activism.

Bediüzzaman stood firm withstanding wrong treatments that have been ever applied for the society, as well as further nationwide complications. He incisively evaluated our century-old maladies, diagnosed the disease, and prescribed the cures, dedicating his entire life to healing, until the day he passed from among us in Urfa. He was always sincere in his words and actions, and brave in expressing his thoughts.

It is not an easy thing to introduce new thoughts and ideas into the collective mind of a society. It is equally difficult to eradicate well-established thoughts, conceptions, and traditions, be they right or wrong. The masses have been under the influence of such residue—useful or not—from the past; individual or collective lives have been shaped accordingly, rejecting everything that is not in conformity with what they are used to, that is not in line with shared feelings. These feelings or preconceptions may not always be appropriate. Considering the fact that collective preconceptions are for the most part deeply rooted, having been experienced and accepted for a long time, then society certainly must be freed from them, being adorned with what is appropriate instead.

Bediüzzaman was always occupied with similar thoughts, from a very young age. He considered it as a disloyalty to his country and his people to conceal even the tiniest truth in this respect; he stood at the mouth of a road and cried out "this is a blind alley" when he saw bad policies jeopardizing the fate of the nation. He was disposed by nature to become agitated when he noticed wrongful things that disfavored religious values. He was a man with a broad vision, and a man of effort; almost tantamount to that of the greatest Prophets. This lion-hearted hero never was able to close his eyes to the devastation of an entire nation. By revealing all the shortcomings and factors that led to our downfall, taking to the deepest ends and most-hidden points, he assisted society in how to perform self-questioning. He frequently reminded us of the reasons behind our decline and produced solutions. He voiced the most painful truths without any doubts; he rode against false preconceptions, rotten thoughts, unbelief, and atheism. Throughout his life he strived to resist the obstacles that hindered the maturing of the epistles of truth.

At the most atrocious times, when nobody dared let slip a word concerning religious truths he alerted the society to the threat of delusion. He waged war against ignorance, poverty, and disunity and shook the foundations of the many anxieties with which society was infatuated. He established a front against atheism and the choking heresy and superstitions at their own impasse. An Arab proverb says "branding is the final remedy." His exceptional civil initiative brought about perfect analysis by placing the burning iron on our centuries-old ostentation. His words echoed in the souls of all, from the royals to the chieftains in the East, from the shayks to the military staff. Although by nature he never enjoyed being venerated, the kind of things he did were "by nature" fascinating for all of society, with all its cross-sections.

The constant jihad, he warned, was to shake off the yoke and chains with which our thoughts and souls were imprisoned. He inspired the young generations with glad tidings of a resurrection, and he guided them to the paths leading to Islamic thought. He was worried that the country would be fragmented, but more than that, narrowing minds, impaired spirits, blind imitation, and modeling on the West severely aroused his concern, as these could lead the nation into all kinds of catastrophes.

He always referred to "knowledge, activating minds, and hard work," and he endeavored to work toward a perfect and affluent society, trying to save individuals from loneliness. For such an ideal he thought "education" was the guidance—education everywhere and at all times—an educational mobilization in which he thought mosques, schools, barracks, streets, playgrounds, and even jails should participate. This was necessary, for with the help of education only can we accomplish a unity in which all minds are focused to the same objective. The company of minds who are not in peace with each other cannot last long. It is preconditioned that consciences join together first, causing hearts and hands to follow suit. This kind of unity is possible only when our life is enjoyed according to religious disciplines which are expounded in the best possible way for contemporary minds, in full deference to the Book, the Sunna, and the pure interpretations of the followers (*salaf al-salihin*).

Our society had to be introduced to the modern age and be reconciled with its meaning and inspirations. We could in no way stay in retreat inside our small shell while the rest of the world was rapidly progressing. To experience the day, one has to bring willpower and endeavor into harmony with the overflowing waterfalls of life. Hopelessly resisting the overwhelming current would result in destruction.

If only a few hundred intellectuals could have embraced Bediüzzaman's messages when he was breathlessly submitting them all over the country, perhaps we could have become one of most affluent and civilized nations of the world today, strong enough to overcome all the obstacles to come and perhaps we would have set about this illumined path at the turn of the 20th century, the illumined path on which we seem to have taken the first steps nowadays, and we would not have had to suffer many of the problems which we have undergone. We are still hopeful, and I would associate those who claim that our society is completely detached from its spiritual roots with indolence and negligence. We cannot deny that our society has fallen like many others have; however, this does not mean that we cannot recover. Predilection for comfort is now being transformed into vigilance, and our souls, once shaken with *harem* thoughts are reviving with freshness. Joyful spring days will surely follow these developments. Bediüzzaman is a good sign for those many heroes like Khidr who will turn our hills into green gardens of worship and Elijah[24] who is to come and set sail for vast oceans.

"The genius does not choose." That is to say, the genius does not make judgments as to whether they would do certain things and would not do others, or claim doing something to be useful or harmful. The genius is a wonder of creation who, like a power source, has gathered all kinds of strength to meet the most complicated, external, esoteric, spiritual, or societal needs of their society, empowered with a divine talent, spiritual impulse and yearning. Observers of his life and works can easily distinguish all aspects of genius in Bediüzzaman. He always maintained his outstanding level, even in his earlier works which indicated the first signs of his exceptional wisdom, and certainly in his later works, which were each a fruit of an agonized lifetime, filled with court cases, imprisonment, and exile.

THE WORLD AWAITED

When we ponder great historical events we can see that thought and action live within one another, that they are interlaced in togetherness; action is, on the one side, planned and fed by thought, while on the other side, new efforts and ventures build the grounds or foundations for new thoughts and projects. In this sense, thought can be seen to be the sky and the rain, the atmosphere and the air for action, while action can be seen to be the container and the flowerpot, the soil and the power of vegetative growth for thought. It cannot be wrong to assume such reciprocity. For every venture is the realization of some thought and plan; every thought is a beginning and a process of finding its true framework and reaching for its target by directing actions toward it. The first stage of willpower is an inner inclination and the last stage is decision, determination, and effort; in this process thought is like the strands of the warp and the weft, from the beginning to the end, and conscious activities are like the patterns and the lace that is woven over those strands. Actions without thought and planning result mostly in fiasco and disorder; thoughts without actions prevent the construction of models—considered to be the latest dimension of thinking—and also damage the spirit of the willpower.

Returning to the present day, not only have the rays of thought been prevented from illuminating all sections of society, but willpower has also been completely paralyzed, representation has been excluded from the system and anarchy has been allowed to kill action. The unfortunate movements of the century have driven the masses from one depression to another, and dragged them into one disorder after another. The masses, in the hands of selfish, greedy, and ambitious souls, have been misled, paralyzed, and confused, and have tottered hither and thither, constantly exploited. Despite all these excuses, we reluctantly can see that the people of today have not yet matured enough to be able to move their own hearts and mental powers, and we say "and yet a bit more. . ." to rid ourselves of the weaknesses in our natural disposition, to strengthen our willpower, to feed our beliefs and to ripen them, and to eradicate all sorts of hopelessness and skepticism from our souls; and also, of course, first of all, to save ourselves from the "Western" shock, we again say "a bit more."

From the industrial revolution in the past to the technological advance of the present day, almost everything has produced shock after shock, creating many complications for us; moreover, the misinterpretation of "scientism" and the flightiness and inconstancy of modernism have largely confused our minds and blurred our vision. Unfortunately, it is highly likely that such weakness and shocks will continue for some time, and our delirious speeches in our somnambulism will apparently persist, and so only God knows how many more years we shall have to bear such a state. We have to and we will endure, for we are conscious of the fact that in order for a society that has been so shocked and shaken to recuperate, come to itself, and to settle its account with the age, disciplined and positive action over a long period of time is needed; like the living patience of corals, a disciplined and active movement that is like the tranquility and constancy of incubation.

After such waiting and action, I truly believe that we will revive and contribute to the betterment and advancement of the world. However, in order to enact such a process we should raise people of great willpower who will give the people of today the newest spirit, people with the profundity of Abd al-Qadir al-Jilani, the breadth of Imam Ghazali, the devoutness of Imam Rabbani, the love and enthusiasm of Mawlana Jalal al-Din Rumi, and the comprehensiveness and composure of Nursi; and who may thus prepare for the people of today fresh ground on which to live. However, it is a fact that we need the time, the conditions and the opportunity to raise such people and thus to break the waves of depression which have been crushing thought and intuition for ages, and to allow the breezes of Judi[25] to blow into the souls of people. Of course, it goes without saying that we need to conquer ourselves, to repair the mechanism of our souls and restore our world of the heart, feelings, and thoughts as well. Otherwise, as we are unable to raise "the cavalry of light," who will help us to reach the fountain of Khidr? As we remain closed to our own values and as long as we, concerning our spiritual systems, live disorientedly, it will not be possible for us to go further and make progress; this has been the case so far. On this issue, we do not need to look for enemies outside, for our enemy is within ourselves, and is watching our misery and vagrancy from his own palace, legs crossed and sniggering at us under his breath.

If we are to produce a strategy for jihad, then this jihad should aim to eradicate the ruthless and faithless enemies enthroned in our hearts, our world has in fact been blockaded for ages by no other than these very enemies. Our people have not been able to raise this fatal blockade and come to themselves, nor to become themselves. Our nation has been like a strange focal point of diverse communities, traditions, and cultures; it has always been a sample of disorder and disorientation and has never pulled itself together, as if it were a victim of thought riven by conflicting allegiances to so many nations, tribes, understandings, and idols; it has knelt to so many false gods at the same time, renewing its solemn oaths before so many false deities everyday. It was so, for, in that unfortunate period, our people never believed that any of the ideas were complete or right. Though it has lived in so many intellectual and ideological cross-currents, our nation has never been able to be completely in or of any of them.

Who knows how many great ideas remained merely latent and inapplicable to life, and what serious projects were trapped and destroyed because of the vague, blurred view of those with myopic vision then? For, in their view, the meaning borne by things and events and the interrelations of humanity, the universe, life, and science are insignificant and meaningless things, not worth dwelling on. Of them, they claimed that we know only what we know about existence; as to what we do not know, this will be solved by the understanding of someone else in the future anyway. Everything is measured, formed, and resolved by their fixed ideas. They can, as the need arises, by showing a world of wrongs to be right and rights to be wrong, go on keeping science, research, and knowledge under the injunctions of their own beliefs and dogmas; and, as if they had even witnessed the whole of creation and its stages from time immemorial, they can brag and swagger in such an assured manner and sell certain hypotheses fait accompli.

If there is no truth to be believed in, if no idea is worth believing or accepting, then what distinguishes existence from chaos? In a world where such an understanding prevails, how can a community be protected from relativism on even improbable matters? Will not the masses steeped in relativism accept what is most true and what is most untrue only to the degree that they accept its opposite? Of course, if such an understanding becomes widespread, everything, from the concept of goodness/badness to the consideration of moral/immoral, will be influenced by relativism. Today, what we need as a nation is a character which is activated by consciousness, realization, and responsibility, a character which is thoughtful in future plans and projects as well as in attitudes and actions concerning the necessities and requirements of today, and which is sincere and uplifted, but balanced; we need a character of thought and spirit which is open to all existence through the heart, one whose mind is cultivated and prosperous, and conscious of knowledge, one who always knows how to renew itself once more, one who is always after order and regularity, and which is quick to repair any damage.

A person of such character will always run from victory to victory. Not, however, in order to ruin countries and set up capitals on the ruins, but rather to move and activate humane thoughts, feelings, and faculties, to strengthen us with so much love, affection, and benevolence that we will be able to embrace everything and everybody, to restore and repair ruined sites, to blow life into the dead sections of society, to become the blood and life and thus flow within the veins of beings and existence and to make us feel the vast pleasures of existence. With all that such a person has, they are a man of God and as His vicegerent they are always in contact with the creation. All their acts and attitudes are controlled and supervised. Everything they do, they do as if it were to be presented for His inspection; they feel by what He feels; they see by His look; they derive their way of speech from His Revelation; they are like the dead man in the hands of the *ghassal*[26] before His Will; their greatest source of power is their awareness of their own weakness, inability, and poverty before Him, and they always try to do their utmost, and not to make a mistake in order to make the best use of that endless treasure.

They are also people of enormous self-accounting and self-control; good and bad, beauty and ugliness are as distinct and ordered within their own places in the mirror of their soul as day and night, light and darkness; all their powers of will, heart, consciousness, and perception are bent on attaining the mechanism of conscience and the highest aims related to and incumbent upon the faculties which compose conscience; knowing "the Almighty Creator's *'atiyya* (gifts, bounties) are carried only (by) the *matiyyas* (the beasts of burden)," in the way responsibility is carried by the willpower, and love by the heart, with the connection and exchange of information between consciousness and existence, and between consciousness and the mysteries behind the veil of existence, with their senses perceiving the absolute truth, without or beyond any manner and measure, without or beyond any quality and quantity, and with their knowledge that places them some steps ahead of the angels, they feel closeness to God.

Regarding their own individual life, their eyes are always on the horizon of being an exemplary person; in the pursuit of excellence they are neck and neck with the saints and sincere friends of God; they are inexpressibly attentive, meticulous, subtle, and particular in fulfilling and representing God's commands. All their attributes, such as their heroic determination to live true Islam, their reaction to the things God does not love, their fearlessness, intrepidity, and perseverance in the way of realizing the precepts of their faith, are beyond our conception or imagination.

Moreover, the enormous breadth of their collective feeling, the depth of their being a person of Truth and simultaneously a fellow of the common person, their love for God and for the creation because of Him, and their ascetic love, joyful zeal, interest and concerns are beyond all measure and expression.

Such a person is indeed, above all, a person of other worldly knowledge and other worldly duty. What we understand by other worldly duty merits a separate discussion.

THE DEVOUT: THE ARCHITECT OF OUR SOULS

Although some people today disdain moral values, the inner depths of the human being, and the importance of the life of the heart and spirit, there is no doubt that the route to true humanity passes through them. No matter what some people may think, the successful application of these dynamics to life offers the only solution that can save the person of the present. People today must be relieved from the social, political, cultural, economic, and various other depressions that are bending them over double, forcing their back into a misshapen twisted form. This deformation has been caused by an onslaught of crises and pressure which have endlessly afflicted the person of today. This vital mission can only be realized by the devout and godly, who never think of themselves, except insofar as they see their own salvation through the salvation of others.

In our view—by which I mean the view of those striving to be truly Muslim—to be saved in the eyes of God depends on the zeal, effort, and perseverance of being a savior. We see that our safety and security in the near and distant future lies in becoming a refuge or sanctuary for other souls, in pumping strength into the willpower of others, and in enlivening the hearts of others; we always want to be among those who face and fight the fire, and who turn their backs on personal or individual interests. The morality of our attitudes and actions is directly related to the consciousness of responsibility, which has been idealized in our spirits.

Such a spirit of responsibility, which almost always exceeds the boundaries of our individuality, forms the nucleus of the order that totally embraces existence and is therefore considered to be the most significant source of universal peace. When this spirit is combined with determined zeal and well-guided willpower, we have achieved the two essentials that are all we need for our salvation. They also speak in an effective voice and an eloquent language that will convey to humanity the spirit and essence or reality it needs.

Those who have turned their backs on existence as a whole and the general order, and who have spent their lives within the dark labyrinth of the ego have never been seen to attain salvation; far from attaining salvation, they have even caused other people, people who held them in high esteem, to perish. The periods in which humanity has made progress have always been those in which we have walked hand in hand with existence. Today, those who plan to walk toward the future should abandon egoism and walk forward wholeheartedly, hand in hand with all things and with every person. Will and ideals will find their true value as long as they are backed by the sincere support of formally constituted bodies, and by closely united zeal, effort, and the collective consciousness. In fact, the only way to become a community while still being an individual, to become a sea while still being a drop of water, and thus to acquire immortality, the only way to make others live and thrive, and to live with them, is to melt away in them and to understand one another, to become friends, fuse, and integrate with them.

From a different perspective, for a person to become a human in the full sense of the word, and to the extent to which we aspire, depends on their being under the command of the heart and on their listening to the soul despite their sensual and bodily concerns and their concern for earning a livelihood (*'aql al-ma'ash*). That is, in order for humans to know themselves and

their surroundings better, they must, to a degree, look at everything and everybody with the eyes of their heart and evaluate
and appreciate them with the criteria of the heart. It should not
be forgotten that a person who has not been able to preserve the
sincerity of their soul and the purity of their heart and who has
not been able to remain as pure and clean as a child, no matter
how great their mental, intellectual, and emotional wealth, no
matter how vast their knowledge, culture, and experience, cannot inspire or inculcate trust in people, nor ever hope to convince them. This is the reason why so many people, except for
those who pretend to believe and trust in someone due to fear,
duress, and oppression, do not believe or trust certain politicians
and those who hold power above logic, reasoning, and heart.
Clean souls and pure hearts have always followed pure thoughts
and honest acts. Clean hearts, which have preserved their innate
purity, as indicated by some blessed words, are considered to be
the place that belongs to Him and where He is known, like a hidden or buried treasure. The divine truth can be perceived and felt
free from any quantity and quality to the extent of the heavenli-
ness and cleanliness of that place. In fact, those who said "I saw
the truth" always mean it in this sense. Carrying a core of *tuba
al-janna*[27] in their hearts, those pure, timeless souls have reached
the gardens of Paradise in this world, a place which everybody
will probably or certainly see in the Hereafter; thus they have
observed the universe in an atom, and are even considered as
having reached the horizon of seeing God beyond that.

Indeed, the hero of the heart is, as the Qur'an and the
Messenger of God have told us, the person of truth, who sees,
thinks, and acts with all the faculties of such a conscience; whose
sitting and standing are mercy, whose words and speech are
mildness and agreement, and whose manners are politeness and
refinement. They are the people of heart and truth who reveal
and teach others the secret of knowing and perceiving the

Creation from the inside, who can express the true meaning and purpose of the Creation. The ultimate goal of such a devout person is vast and very important, namely to carry every soul to eternal life, to offer everyone the elixir of eternity, and by escaping completely from their self, their personal interests, and their concerns for the future, they are able to be either in the depths of their self and inner world, or to be in the objective world, or to be in their world of the heart,or to be in the presence of their Creator, and to observe and retain such significant and diverse relations all at the same time. Despite their own physical and material needs or poverty, they are a keen volunteer and altruist, and are always occupied and preoccupied with planning the happiness of the people around them. They are always developing for the community in which they live projects of peace, prosperity, and welfare, like the beautifully expanding patterns of embroidery. In the face of the sufferings and miseries experienced by their community and the whole of humanity, with a heart similar to one of God's messengers, they endure palpitations, exasperation, and pangs of conscience.

They therefore struggle with the evil surrounding their own people and the whole world. While fighting it off, they do not engage in describing and reporting vain and idle things, because such description "leads astray and corrupts pure minds," but rather become restless, anxious, and take great pains to produce and implement projects that will resolve matters. They are heroes of Prophet-like resolution who tackle and overcome problems with a very serious love of duty, a very strong feeling of responsibility, and God-consciousness of restraint (*ihsan*[28]). A hero of resolution soars with the wings of weakness, helplessness, humility, and poverty, is always taut and ready for release, like the string of a longbow, with the joyful zeal of gratitude, and feels deeply the pain of responsibility and accountability for reviving universal harmony and truth. Their responsibility is such that whatever enters an individual's comprehension and conscious willpower never remains outside of theirs: responsibility for the creation and events, nature and society, the past and the future, the dead and the living, the young and the old, the literate and the illiterate, administration and security . . . everybody and everything. And of course they feel the pain of all these responsibilities in their heart; they make themselves felt as maddening palpitations, exasperation in the soul, always competing for their attention. It seems to me that this is the sort of resolve that is attributed to God's messengers, which makes people strive for that which is valued above all values in the eyes of God and which makes them acquire ascension of the soul and closeness to their Lord.

The pain and distress that arises from the consciousness of responsibility, if it is not temporary, is a prayer, a supplication which is not rejected, and a powerful source of further alternative projects, and the note most appealing to consciences which have remained clear and uncorrupted. Every person of spirit has the potential to exceed their own power and that of their community in proportion to the vastness of their pain, and can become a focal point for the strength and power of past and future generations. Let me remind you of the necessity here to differentiate between those who live and those who make others live. What we are always stressing is that it is those who live their lives in sincerity, loyalty, and altruism at the expense of their own selves in order to make others live who are the true inheritors of the historical dynamics to whom we can entrust our souls. They do not ever desire that the masses follow them. Yet their existence is such a powerful, inevitable invitation that all run to them, wherever they are, as if these devout people were a centre of attraction.

The future will be the work of these devout people who can represent such a significant mission, showing their responsibility and exhibiting their accomplishments. The existence and continuance of our nation and the nations related to us will be permeated with the thoughts, inspirations, and outcomes of a new civilization and with the vast, reviving dynamism of a rich culture, carried aloft into the future on the shoulders of these devout people. They are the trustees of the sublime truths and the heirs of our historical riches.

What is meant by the heirs of history is to be the heir to all the accumulation—the known and the unknown, the great and the small—of the past, and to make use of and increase that accumulation in order to produce new compounds and a new synthesis; later to convey all these safely to the future generations, the true owners. If the devout do not fulfill the historic task of today and tomorrow, then they will have ruined today and wasted all our tomorrows. This responsibility is such that if the heir is lazy, heedless, negligent, or indifferent to it, or if they search for someone else to assign or transfer it to, or if they even start to long for the higher realms instead of their current task, because they have been attracted by the beauties of the Hereafter, then they will have betrayed the cause and history, and thus destroyed the bridges between us and the future. Rather, for our existence and its continuance, it is necessary, indeed vital, for us to look to the future and consider that the future will be ours, as such a view is extremely important for the function and effectiveness of our action to keep it as a headline above our feelings, thoughts, and plans. The alternative to this is to be disrespectful to our nation, to betray it. It is high time we supported all our institutions in all the fields of science, art, economy, family, morality, and religion, and we reinforced and raised them to the highest levels that they have yet been in history, as is their due. And we are looking forward to the arrival of such people of will, resolution, effort, and zeal.

We are not in need of local or foreign grants, favors or ideologies. We need the physicians of thought and spirit who can arouse in all people the consciousness of the value of responsibility, sacrifice, and suffering for others; who can produce mental and spiritual depth and sincerity in the place of promises of passing happiness; who can, with a single attempt, make us reach the point of observing the beginning and the end of creation.

Now we are waiting, looking forward to the arrival of these people who have so much love for their responsibility and cause that, if necessary, they would even give up entering Paradise; people like this, if they have already entered, would then seek ways of leaving Paradise. Like Muhammad, the Messenger of God, who said, "If they placed the sun in my right and the moon in my left to abandon my cause, I would not until God made the truth prevail or I died in the attempt." This is the horizon of God's Messenger. Bediüzzaman Said Nursi, a scholar exuberant with the rays that emanate from God's Messenger, bent double by the pain of his cause said, "In my eyes I have neither love for Paradise nor fear for Hell, and if I saw the faith of my people secure, I would be ready now to be burned in hell-fire." Likewise, Abu Bakr opened his hands and prayed in a way that would shake the heavens, "O my Lord, make my body so great that I alone fill up Hell and thus no place may be left for anyone else."

Humanity is terribly in need of people with inner depths and sincerity now, more than anything else, for people who suffer and cry for the sins and errors of others; who look forward to forgiveness and pardon of others before their own; who, instead of entering Paradise and taking their pleasures individually there, prefer to stay in the *A'raf*[29] and from there try to take all the people to Paradise along with them; and who, even if they enter Paradise, will not be able find time to enjoy the pleasures of Paradise because of their thoughts for others and their concern to save them from the hell-fire.

THE CONSCIOUSNESS OF RESPONSIBILITY

The most deeply significant aspect of existence is action and effort. Inertia is dissolving, decomposition, and another name for death. Connecting or relating action to responsibility gives action its primary humane dimension. An action or effort which is not disciplined by responsibility cannot be considered to be complete.

Most human beings pursue various goals and objectives. However, unless this pursuit gains depth through responsibility, it is vain to expect anything of value in consequence. Nevertheless, the self-seeking, whose heads are turned by greed for personal interest and profit, work incessantly; politicians visit everywhere and deliver their enthralling speeches; the media produce a huge range of shows in the name of informing the public; some circles of society turn to indulgence with every breath the year round; some so-called religious men are driven by a desire for profit, and stock exchange indexes fall and rise with speculations day and night; some state offices shower favors only to particular ideologies and their adherents; and some wise men watch these numerous happenings with the utmost indifference. That is, as the mighty and the oppressors oppress, and the oppressed and crushed accept all these as "ordinary," as "natural selection, the survival of the fittest," so many things which need to be done become harder to do.

> *It is wrong if they say a society can live with such insensitivity,*
> *Show me a nation, which has survived with a dead spirituality?*
>
> Mehmed Akif Ersoy

And should you happen to ask such people, "Where are you heading?" they either ignore you or reproach you and continue on their way. If they do not slap or spit in your face, they will most probably respond by ignoring or mocking the consciousness of responsibility as in, "Every sheep is hung by its leg,"[30] or "He who saves the ship is the captain."[31] Even with the utmost insolent, free and easy behavior, causing palpitations in our alert conscience, they respond nonsensically, "Long live the snake that does not bite me." Alas, you can face many responses like this that will clash with your purest thoughts and most innocent feelings.

However, even though these are not the thoughts of believing and sensitive hearts, it is not reconcilable with our consciousness of responsibility to say "stuff and nonsense" and to pass by. For we, as an entire nation, are surrounded by enemies and enmities. As long as we are under such a siege, we cannot even claim to be ourselves with respect to our feelings, thoughts, faith, art, and free enterprise; we cannot thus retain or protect our Islamic dignity, our national honesty, save our ship and reach the shore in safety, establish our own world, live as we wish, become the inheritors of the Earth and reach God. It is time for us to open our eyes and see reality, to use our insight and stand as the protector and patron of what our accomplishments and purge ourselves of whatever is gnawing at our being and personality from the inside. Otherwise, one day it will be impossible to retain even what we have now.

Once, our enemies used to be ignorance, illiteracy, poverty, disunion, and bigotry. Now to these have been added cheating, bullying and coercion, extravagance, decadence, obscenity, insensitivity, indifference, and intellectual contamination. May those who preserve their purity of religion, clarity of thought, and patriotic feeling, and those who share concerns similar to those I have stated above, excuse my saying that for quite a long time now our younger generations and some of the simple-minded among the older generation have been led astray by virtue of their naïveté; they have been deceived by corrupt ideologies, the only merits of which lie in their elaborate presentation. Even if this is true only in some circles, to experience such a deviation of thought and personality as a nation would be the veritable invasion of this blessed country. In fact, only then Sultan Mehmed the Conqueror would be poisoned, Sultan Murad I stabbed, Sultan Yıldırım Bayezid died of grief, and Sultan Yavuz Selim afflicted by a tumor. This is nothing less than the massacre of the spirit of the nation which emerged victorious from the National War; a massacre led by the evil of the age, by the heedlessness of the intelligentsia, and the indifference of the masses.

We are charged with the responsibility for endowing our world with a fresh, new spirit, woven from a love of faith, a love of our fellow human being, and a love of freedom. We have further been charged with the responsibility for being ourselves, connected to the principle of these three loves, and for preparing the ground for the shoots, the pure roots of the blessed tree of Paradise, so that it will be nurtured and grow in the loam of these loves. This, of course, depends on the existence of heroes who will take responsibility for and protect the country's destiny and the history, religion, traditions, culture, and all sacred things that belong to the people; this will depend on heroes who are absolutely full of a love for science and knowledge, burgeoning with the thought of improvement and construction, sincere and devout beyond measure, patriotic and responsible, and, therefore, always conscientiously at work, in charge, and on duty. Thanks to these heroes and their sincere efforts, our system of thoughts and understanding and the fruit of these will prevail with our people; the sense of devoting oneself to others and to the community will gain prominence; the understanding of the division of labor, the management of time, and assisting and liaising with one another will be revived; all relationships of authority-subject, employer-employee, landlord-tenant, landowner-peasant, artist-admirer, attorney-client, teacher-student will become different aspects of the unity of the whole; all this will come about once more and all our expectations from ages past will come true, one by one. We now live in an era in which our dreams are being realized and we believe that with good timing each of the responsibilities of the age will have been accomplished by the time its day arrives.

That is the basis of our dreams and vision; the first and principle way to realize them is through the consciousness and the ethic of responsibility. As complete inertia is a death and disintegration, and irresponsibility in action is disorder and chaos, we are left with no alternative but to discipline our actions with responsibility. Indeed, all our attempts should be measured by responsibility. Our way is the way of truth, our cause is to hold and raise the truth, and our target is to seek the pleasure of God in each and every blinking of the eye. In fact, to be so is the alms we pay for being human and the reason and justification for our willpower. We hold ourselves obliged to seek the goal of life in our lives, to awaken to love in our souls, to comprehend the consciousness of responsibility in our conscience, to show the route to science, knowledge, art, morality, and wisdom to those who are ready for reception to the source of a system whose principles, foundations, light, and driving force are faith and love; we hold ourselves as servants who will not accept release from this mission. Our efforts, which we hope to bring to fruition in the line and spirituality of all the friends of God—the saints (*awliya*), the sincere (*asfiya*), the good (*abrar*), and the close (*muqarrabin*)—will be the beginning of a second Renaissance.

So far, every age has had its wonder: the rebirth of humanity in the sixth century, the revival of the Turkish tribes and nations by Islam in the tenth century, and the metamorphosis in the province of Söğüt of a small chrysalis into the magnificent Ottoman butterfly. I suppose the wonder of the twenty-first century will appear to be that our people and the peoples related to us will attain their rightful place in the international balance of power. Such an emergence, which will change the flow and direction of the history of the world, will rotate about the axis of the soul, morality, love, and virtue. Through the spiritual struggle (jihad) which we can also call "a struggle for knowledge, morality, truth, and justice," we believe that the generations which have so far been left without protection and ideals will experience a new resurrection in a manner like the exhilaration of reaching the banner of the Prophet in the field of resurrection, the banner under which all Muslims will gather.

FROM CHAOS TO ORDER - I

For several centuries, with respect to our understanding of morality, virtue, science, and knowledge, our society has had the appearance of a wreck. It has been searching for an alternative system of order and thought in education, art, and morality. In fact, we need genius minds with iron wills that are able to carry the title of vicegerent of God on Earth, and which are able to intervene in events and challenge the orphan spirit and puny thought which attach no importance to the consciousness of responsibility, humane values, knowledge, morality, true contemplation, virtue, and art in such a vast territory, we need refined minds and an iron will which will embrace and interpret creation in its depth and entirety and humanity in all its worldly and other-worldly vastness.

Recent gusts of change and transformation in the world tore the masks from the faces of many and revealed their true identities; they also momentarily lifted the veil from our eyes, and thus the true essence of everybody and everything became clear to our view. Nowadays, we can observe events taking place around us more clearly and draw sounder, more reliable conclusions. Consequently, we have now deduced and realized that it is not only our external appearance and attire, our way of thinking and our philosophy of life that were subjected to the mishap of being exiled, forsaken and obliterated from memory, but also our national culture, the consciousness of history, the system of morality, acceptance, and the interpretation of virtue, the understanding of art and the roots of spiritual essence—these were no less subjected to erosion. In fact, they suffered rather more. All our spiritual bonds were shredded, the sources of virtue dried up, and in their place impassable cliffs and abysses were thrown between us and our past.

In this blessed world of ours, we have experienced periods in which the intellectuals were silenced; the fount of thought was sealed; those who represented might and authority reinforced the deviation and degeneration; the poor, unfortunate generations were always trapped "in the most lifeless, hopeless, and darkest feelings, within a groaning chaos, like the dead."

In this "red" period, when everywhere was pervaded by the thick dust and smoke of hopelessness, eyes shed tears of helplessness, hearts sighed when looking toward the faces that did not know shame, lamenting their feelings with a voice from their deepest self, bemoaning: "What else could you expect from those confused, who sailed forth into atheism; from those unthinking people, who praise and applaud everybody and everything; from those victims of their deeply sullied conscience, who are accustomed to bowing to that power?" However, not a single one of all those things that were shaken and demolished, which perished and disappeared has been replaced. And now, witnessing the unease, the discomfiture that we have started to feel recently in all of our hearts, even deep in the hearts of the so-called realists, who know nothing but the pursuit of their own pleasure, it has become crystal clear that nothing has been built or established in place of what was demolished, what perished and disappeared; the values of society have been left inverted.

Now let me ask you earnestly how and with what we should overcome this moral misery, which has turned life into a burden and an enigma, and how should we overcome the crises which form an ever stronger and deeper whirlpool in ourselves as the days pass? How can we tackle, surmount, and extricate ourselves from these individual, familial, and social crises? How can we walk confidently toward the future? With a few imported fantasies and fancy ideologies? Or with the limited reasoning of this age on which they try to build everything? No! Neither those illegitimate thoughts and ideologies nor that dark logic are able to rise from under such a heavy burden.

All the efforts of reformation in our world remain nothing but artifice; they have never successfully pursued an objective nor reached even the smallest target. Those at the top, paintbrush in hand, have assumed that it was a skill, or perhaps even revolutionary, to daub paint over the wounds that appeared on the national and social body; yet they have been blind to the internal bleeding in the major blood vessels of the vital organs and the complications caused by that bleeding. Since the turn of the century, with the exception of some success in the private sphere and the achievements of the heroes of our National War, everything has continued on this way. Furthermore, it is impossible even to claim that the blessed effort of our heroes has been continued with a purity and strength comparable to that shown at its origin. Today, it is not impossible, but it is very difficult, to talk of unity on such a scale and to imagine such a rising and revival.

Although different groups have separated and distanced themselves more and more from others, they do not acknowledge clearly the substantial differences among them concerning their intellectual lives, spirit, and essence. They have become alienated from one another to an extraordinary extent and behave like beasts attacking each other. This has reached such a level that if one says something is black, the other contradicts him and claims that it is white; if one puts forward an idea, the other opposes and refutes it; one considers the alternative ideas of the other as being treacherous; and one sees the firmness of the other as bigotry and fanaticism. Apart from all this contrariness, now imagine the dimensions of this fight, or rather, brawl, where there are no criteria commonly or mutually acknowledged by all. Try now to discover on which side the truth is to be found.

That is why, more than anything else today, we need a way of thinking which is undeceiving and criteria which are not misleading on the way that carries us to truth and virtue. While our conscience and our moral and ethical values could once have been considered to be a source of light sufficient to resolve many problems, unfortunately today that conscience has been wounded and those moral values are scattered in confusion; both of these important dynamics have been uprooted and, like ancient fountains in museums, their source or spring has dried up. In the words of M. Akif Ersoy:

> What elevates morality is neither knowledge nor conscience,
> Fear of God is the real source of all virtue and excellence.

If you add to all this the fact that willpower has slackened as far as possible, that reasoning has become as shameless as possible, and that human feelings are as wicked and ferocious as fiends, the depth and vastness of the nightmare we have been experiencing will be self-evident.

It is therefore essential to start by revising once more all the fundamentals of our reasoning, finding the line of logical thinking, giving our willpower its due, and raising resolute generations. As we are living in a universe besieged by causes, we cannot ignore them. Negligence of causes in a world of causes is absolute determinism and deviation. To become responsible and accountable does not demand that we ignore causes, but rather renders our observance of the principle of causes (*tanasub al-illiyat*) as an indispensable requirement.

Departing from this point, if we do not, with serious intent, analyze today the fundamentals of those particular harmful thoughts, ideologies, and movements, and if we do not take the necessary measures against them, it is inevitable that we will again live through similar miserable morality, social disasters, deviations, and corruptions, all in their different scales and dimensions. It is not commendable that we know the consequences of a disaster after it has already taken place. The merit is to foresee and predict which causes and factors produce what effect. It is even difficult to show such hindsight or wisdom concerning our recent history; we can never claim that we gave our willpower its due at any time. Quite the contrary, within that twilight period our people were suspicious of their own thought, willpower, and resolution and thus always sought some superior and extraordinary willpower to govern them. Moreover, by means of the thought of such and such a "scholar," "scientist," "country," or "state" lack of character was inculcated into the pure consciousnesses and innocent consciences of our people, and thus their resolution and perseverance were shackled. In time, the dominance and rule of these people over our thoughts and acts caused a variety of deviations of personality, dizziness, deviations of reasoning, distortions and contradictions in our thinking, our acceptance of ideas and interpretations. This then brought about some terrible deformations in those who surrendered, without terms and conditions, such people and thought. However, none but the Divine Will ought to be believed in and accepted without inspection and criticism.

Descartes said, "Thought which is not free cannot be considered thought." Are we not at least able to think as Descartes in order to save ourselves from the scholasticism of today which is already rotten and outmoded in many respects? Alas, it seems not . . .

In coming years, the generations who can see the bright horizons of this world and the next will revise the thoughts, formulas, and systems which were imported to us and formed inside us, they will purify society from alienating and filthy things and affairs, and connect it with its own spiritual roots, so that it can protect and preserve its essence, its personality, and walk its own line to its own future. Yet while walking it will remain so intimate with the world that it will be able to read and study yesterday together with today, one within the other, so that it does not merely discard the past because it is old and blindly accept the things it considers new and fresh. The most obvious characteristic of this enlightened generation will be to know everything related to the past and present, to realize that what is commonly assumed to be known is not at all what we know to be true, and, in one way or another, to try to understand the truth along with the findings of laboratories by sieving all through the filter of mind, logic, and reason and by heeding the currents of inspiration.

To achieve such an improvement and change it is vitally important to know our near past, its heroes, and historic personalities: in the formation of our history, who were the most influential persons, and what were the most influential factors, motives and reasons? Who are the people who have most recently revived the love and enthusiasm of our people? Who composed and performed the works which reflect our national, social, and spiritual beauties? Once we know all this, I think we may understand better what we need to envision and how to present our plans for the future clearly. Thus we may attain the happiness of walking in the footsteps of the heroes who kept safe and sound in their hearts their thought, cause, love, and tolerant morality.

FROM CHAOS TO ORDER - II

The harmony between creation and natural phenomena is predestined; the order among men is voluntary or by free will and to a great extent has its origins in love and fear. Order is another name for peace, satisfaction, and societal harmony, as well as a promising future. As there is no peace and harmony in chaos, it is not possible to talk about the future or efficiency in anarchic circumstances.

At first sight, order seems to be the product of simple willpower and mind isolated from belief; yet the mind which is not under the control of the soul, and the willpower which is not able to cut the roots of evil tendencies and incite inclinations for good are considered to be more on the side of anarchy than with order.

All creation, apart from humanity, has always maintained in order since the world came into existence. An enthralling order prevails everything and everywhere, from the harmonious movements of electrons and atoms to the splendid design of flowers, from the balance and harmony between the living and non-living to the stars which twinkle and wink at us and flow like a poem and emotion from deep space into our hearts, from the meanings represented in the flowers, leaves, and branches of the plants and trees to the life that breathes vitality in and out.

If the conscience observes and evaluates the book of creation for an instant, it observes and perceives the order and harmony that emanates everywhere, the fascinating beauty and awe-inspiring richness of essence in everything. It does not require a very profound sensitivity; a heart even with very little, or limited, sensitivity can feel, sense, perceive a poem—chanting and reciting in the tones and tunes of infinity—in every form, pattern, color, voice, and sound, from the harmonious, pleasant warbling of the birds to the terrifying, awe-inspiring, thunder of lightning flashes, from the colorful, delicate, vibrant patterns of flowers to the mysterious lights of the stars and sky. And those who are one step ahead of the others, those who know, observe what is performed by means of physics, chemistry, biology, and astrophysics. From the awe-inspiring depths of the sea, from its tumultuous waves to the cool tranquility of the paradisiacal glades in the woods, from the dignified standing of the hills to the unreachable, insurmountable majestic peaks of the mountains, from the continuous flow and ripple of water to the depths of the sky stretching to infinitude, everything says order and harmony, and cries out the vast meanings in the spirit of the creation.

So, if order is imbued in everything and everywhere, where did this chaos, which we will call disorder, irregularity, and illegality, come from? The world came to know chaos and the immorality behind it through human beings: the human beings who did not surrender their minds to God, who were unable to slam on the brakes of their willpower and to stimulate their feelings for the good. Humans are creatures vulnerable to a great variety of ambitions and they have a greater number and variety of weaknesses than other creatures. The emotions of destruction, feelings of anarchy, and eddies of disorder are manifest in different frequencies in almost all our weaknesses, such as greed, ambition, anger, hatred, malice, violence, and lust. It is impossible for humanity to save itself from the negative consequences of these without taking control of all the evil feelings; this can only be done by virtue of being cultivated, well-mannered, and well-educated. We cannot save ourselves until we invigorate and consolidate our humane feelings, until we say yes to a tacit social contract in our conscience by taking into consideration the existence of others in our wishes and desires, our joys and sorrows, and our freedoms and rights.

The education which will raise humans from potential humanity to true humanity must be directed toward the Divine and by the Divine, and it must be based around the gifts and talents that have been bestowed by God. Our culture should be fed on the roses grown in our own ground and on the nectar that emanates from our roots of spirit and essence; thus it will not create any adverse reaction or criticism from the collective conscience or the verdict of history. The social contract should be realized according to the conditions and requirements of the age and within a framework of the most advanced rights and freedom, so that the different sections and circles of the society do not lose their power, authority, respect, credit, self-esteem, or nominal value within a tangle of opposition, nor be caught up within the vicious circle of neutralizing one another with contradictions. What we mean by the contract here is not a collective contract on paper with so many people's signatures adorning the foot of the page, but a contract which is related to and limited by respect for the concept of rights and freedom and by love for the truth, on the part of people who have awakened to the humane values in their consciences.

The limit and the framework of this contract is defined by the structure of the individual's heart, the vastness of their spirit and the realization that their faith and what they believe in constitute one part of their nature or disposition. That is why the contract of each person's conscience corresponds to their level of humane feeling. A community which is composed of mature individuals, who have overcome corporeality with respect to their heart and spiritual lives, is one which is in exemplary order. Such order in the world of humanity is permanent and promising for the future, as it is a dimension of the universal harmony that encompasses the whole of creation.

In our world, the state is like the captain on the bridge of the ship whose crew is made of merits, virtues, and morality. This captain's duty is to employ and make the best of the crew under his authority, to establish harmony and concord among them and with the order of the universe, and thus make them reach the destination and attain their goals without having them collide with the crushing waves of events. As it is impossible to produce a healthy society and a perfect state from a community whose members are deprived of virtues and who wallow in the abysses of immorality, so too is it misleading and self-deluding to expect the masses of disorder and chaos, which is attacked on all sides by some disease, to be promising for the future. It is therefore a mistaken conjecture, an illusion and a baseless consolation to expect something significant in the name and fields of administration and security from the masses merely from their dark fortune, no matter what their names and forms are. Both authority and state can only be well-established through targeting a high ideal which will give life to and maintain it within the society, planning everything according to that ideal and if every effort and action can be referred, ascribed and reduced to "One."

Every individual and every vital unit should be prepared and should plan to carry or raise all the people to the summit so that small interests, schemes, and accounts within individual plans cannot spoil the general harmony, and so that different circles or groups cannot be born, swell, clash, and dissolve within and at the expense of one another, like the waves of the sea. Once, as the spirit of Islam prevailed over the whole of life, this objective was defined and established so well that the members and units which constituted society were each made a pillar of order, and thus the walk to the summits was achieved as if within the natural course of life.

The biggest gift of today's generations to the world of tomorrow is the act of revising our idea of order, of renewing the belief that the Divine harmony within creation will be carried to the world of humanity by means of our willpower, and of pulling the balance of nations into this axis. For such an important mission it will be enough, I believe, to review once more our own willpower, to establish and ascertain our place in the eye of God, to set the targets for our people and nation, to consolidate sound, logically consistent, strategies and policies, and to realize or bring to life the dynamics we already possess.

THE MAJOR CAUSE OF OUR PEOPLE

The whole world is now moving toward spring. Despite problems in the past, almost everyone agrees that the future is bright. Rather than dwelling on this phenomenon though, it is more important to consider the state of those who exert their resolution, willpower, and high performance in order to achieve this future. To think of the future of one's country and nation is undoubtedly the duty of every intelligent and enlightened individual. However, I cannot say for sure whether everyone is conscious that they bear such a responsibility. What I know is that a handful of people in our country over the years have lived day and night, continuously working for and being preoccupied by aspirations for the future, and used, spent, and sacrificed everything they have had in the hope that one day the road they are building will reach the level plains.

This country and land, for which millions of people once sacrificed their lives in a variety of ways, is in an exciting time of a passage from the past to the future, accompanied by so many loyal children; this has happened once before, and this country and its people are now full of hope and deeply conscious of and enthusiastic about the idea of the advancement of their people. This is true to such an extent that when they are carrying out daily, mundane work with one hand and foot, then they are trying to produce plans and projects for the future with the other hand and foot, using their feelings and consciousness that are given over to the disposal and command of their ideals. So we can say the major cause which this honorable and majestic his-

tory and fortunate and glorious nation of ours has been defending and protecting, a cause which has formed and developed for
over a thousand years, is once more starting to kindle in the
spirits with a deep emotion; an emotion like homesickness and
a longing for return. Many of today's generations, with their
consciousness of union and solidarity, their determination and
perseverance to make their own nation the number one nation
of the era, seem to be both evidence to this cause and the representatives of this mission. Unless an opposing wind blows and
scatters everything, it seems that the future will be theirs.

This cause was spread by the first great men of Islam to the
four corners of the world over a very short time, and gained a
different momentum with the Umayyads and Abbasids, a different value with the Seljuks, and finally with the Ottomans
became a matter of the highest importance, although it was also
subjected to great inauspiciousness over a certain period. It has
once more started to be experienced as a process that goes from
village to city, family to state, street to school, art to science,
work to morality, and thanks to those who have awakened the
country with the excitement and enthusiasm of their hearts and
who have colored and watered the map of the country with their
continuous tears. Therefore, despite everything, the faint and
predictable light of dawn has started to appear gradually, send-
ing its light everywhere. In a sense, although we have been subjected to the deception of false dawns over and over again, it is
those false dawns which are the most reliable witnesses that the
sun will soon rise.

During that unfortunate period, issues such as greed for the
material, love of position, passion for life, desire for fame, and
desire to hold on to the world, came and occupied the place of
our intellectual and spiritual causes, and the lowest things were
consecrated. However, now the spirit and essence—or reality—
are directing in charge, and things have started to resume their

place. Instead of the immature thoughts and fantasies of that time, which boasted their claim to save the country and advance it to the level of Western standards—a claim which appeared to be true, but which was in fact no more than idle posturing—there are now, in huge numbers, lofty representatives—or candidates soon-to-be—of science, knowledge, art, morality, and virtue who are inheritors of all the values of our glorious past.

Meanwhile, it is true that there are ruthless battles going on in the fields of politics, the arenas of interests, and at the turnstiles of profit; some brag, "Let's save the country," "Let's enlighten our people," "Let's advance our nation." We always pay the penalty for the whims and passions of those who have concocted stories that mislead the people, leading the nation into chaos. However, I earnestly ask you: Is it possible to show that there was ever any period during which such things did not take place or exist? Such things have always existed, and will always exist, today and tomorrow. History is not the history of good people only. Along with the history of good people is the history of those who swear, bite, gnaw, trap, betray, and accuse one another. You do not have to go far to find it. If we look back at our recent past, we will see this, and we will shiver at how many times souls were assassinated in the name of democracy, how many times the different sections of society were turned into wolves to devour one another, and how many times our hearts were made to drink hatred, malice, and resentment.

Looking at some sections of society from the perspective of some matters, the things we have been doing today will not be different from those of yesterday, and tomorrow's actions will be no different from those of today. In even the purest and the most ideal societies, there have existed, and will exist, some dark souls who continually cheat and deceive, thus dividing, exploiting, and oppressing, and who continually change the masks on their faces and are thus able to conceal themselves and their true identity. On the other hand, apart from such people, there most certainly exists a world of positive people and positive efforts.

Today the movement for education has been realized under various names and titles, and the efforts for love, tolerance, and dialogue are indeed important attempts toward bringing the parts of society together and making the sources of its spiritual power move and function; and they are indeed sufficient within the hands of the generations whose metaphysical-spiritual tension is complete and who really believe, to re-float the nation's ship, a ship which has run aground, and cause it to sail safely on. There is no doubt that today's generations, who have been ill-treated and misused as regards their spirit and character, and who have suffered great losses one after another in their morality, virtue, thinking, art, indeed, in all general human values, will reach a new resurrection thanks to their spiritual freedom and intellectual stability.

The nineteenth and twentieth centuries became an age of disintegration and going backward for us. For a long time, the true reasons for this were not perceived and the views on this were deliberately distorted. Therefore masterpieces of real backwardness were produced and displayed in religion, science, art, and aesthetics, and in time, some currents occasionally in the form of conflicts of ideas turned out to be the currents of rejection and atheism. These conflicts of ideas arose due to fantasy and confusion. This was true to such an extent that in the place of scientific genius, jugglery and trickery, instead of enlightenment, illusion, and instead of struggle and perseverance, defamation became fashionable. Those who considered deceit to be a skill exerted all their energy and efforts and strove to bring down historical truths through fabrication, willful misrepresentation, deceit, slander, and malicious instigation. Look at the manifestation of the Divine Destiny on which those historical dynamics and the spiritual roots of the people are still standing, and contrast this with how the deceitful ones who have fallen and gone have themselves become.

This nation awakening to the path of the Prophet once more, like the snowdrops everywhere dancing in the spring winds, is whispering the songs of newest existence, of freshest revival. We seem today to be more lively, agile, and determined with the hope, ease, and cheerfulness of the realization of finding and coming to ourselves; I wish that our every effort henceforth, every tear we shed, may become the remedy for our grievous wounds and the light of the tomorrows which seem so dark!

Having entered the twenty-first century, the future of the nations related to us can be considered to be under the trusteeship of the doves of the army of light soaring on the wings of light; these, in turn, are now considered to be the representatives of science, knowledge, virtue, and morality. We hope these blessed generations a great majority of whom have dedicated themselves to teaching and education, will be our guides with the voice of light and with the thought of light, and will not only make us regain all the historical values we have lost, but also enable our people settle their accounts with the era.

Indeed, the cause and goal of our existence has nothing at all to do with might or force. Recognizing that the power which has surrendered and submitted to the Truth has its own reason for existence, we wholeheartedly acknowledge and respect the necessity for techniques and technology, the necessity and immediacy for industry, the value of science and knowledge. In addition to these, there is the vast perspective of our thought, our outstanding acceptance and interpretation of art, and our understanding of the implementation of true justice, which is meticulously sensitive, and also our belief in the obligation for our country to be nurtured and supported by these. Therefore, we need today, more than anything, well-bred minds, vast perspectives, and spiritual teachers with broad horizons who can establish due balance of all these, for and on behalf of our country and people, who can raise our nation and people to the apex of thought, who can direct us to the roots of our essence or spirit, and who can provide opportunities for, and give a start to our souls that are in need of, and in love with, the Sublime.

Rather than party politics or cliquishness, our country needs disciples of knowledge, morality, and virtue who are well-equipped with faith and hope, full of enthusiasm, and who have divested themselves of any wish, desire, and distress, be it material or immaterial, pertaining to this world or the other. Until we can find them and put ourselves in their hands, this intertwined exile and slavery, though relative, seems set to continue. We beseech the Owner of Infinite Mercy to send soon the long awaited generations to our aid, with those consoling signs which we have already seen appear on the horizon.

IDEAL GENERATIONS

On the eve of the beautiful days of the future, days whose dawns are breathing festivities, it is clear that we face crises that seem insurmountable. Like social troubles, national problems, and natural disasters, the crises that besiege a society cannot be overcome or resolved by mundane measures. Solutions for such crises depend on insight, knowledge, and wisdom becoming widespread. It is of no use—indeed, it is a mere waste of time—to try to solve such crises with aimless, limited, unpromising policies that are like mundane political maneuvers. From the past to the present, people of spirit, essence, and insight have resolved the commonest and most widespread depressions and crises with their immense horizons and zeal with unimaginable ease by using and activating the present day sources of power for the future. Some laypeople suppose that their own ingenious measures are super-human and have admired and marveled at them as such. However, all they are doing, like all other successful people, is to use fully and efficiently the capacity, talents, and opportunities granted them by Almighty God.

People of discernment are always, in all their acts and manners, busy and preoccupied with plans and projects for today and tomorrow; they use all they have and all possibilities and opportunities as material to build the bridge to cross over to the future; and they always feel the pain and distress of carrying today onto tomorrow; to resolve the problems depends, to a certain extent, on overcoming or passing over the present time, and in fact being beyond time. That is, being able to see, fore-see, and evaluate today and tomorrow in the same way. You can call such scope of thought, which entails embracing tomorrow from today and comprehending the future's spirit and essence and content, an "ideal," if you so wish. One who does not have such a horizon can neither overcome a multitude of problems nor promise anything for tomorrow. Even though some simple people have assumed great proportions like these, the pomp, circumstance, and magnificence of the Pharaohs, Nimrods, Caesars, and Napoleons, their noisy and hectic lives, which bedazzled so many, never became, and can never become, prom-ising for the future in any way. For those people were the poor, the wretched, who subjugated truth to the command of might, who always sought social ties and congruity around self-interest and profit, and who lived their lives as slaves, never accepting freedom from spite, selfishness, and sensuality.

In contrast, first the Four Rightly-Guided Caliphs and later the Ottomans presented such great works, whose consequences exceed this world and reach to the next, that these works are in essence able to compete with the centuries; of course, only for those who are not beguiled by temporary eclipses. Although they lived their lives and duties fully and passed away, they will always be remembered, talked of, and find a place in our hearts as the good and the admirable. In every corner of our country, the spirit and essence of such people as Alparslan, Melikşah, Osman Gazi, Fatih, and many others, waft like the scent of incense, and hopes and glad tidings flow into our spirits from their vision.

Caesar trampled down the ideal of Rome with his whims and desires; Napoleon imprisoned and killed the ideal of Great France in the net of his greed and ambitions; and Hitler con-sumed the aim of Great Germany with his rash madness. On the other hand, the ideal, which is open to continuity, of our people, whose heroism expresses integrity and continuousness, has always been held high and above all meanness or vulgarity, whether in victory or defeat; it is held dear, beloved, sacred, and highly esteemed, like a banner for whose sake lives are given. Under such a banner, Fatih walked through Constantinople, Süleyman the Magnificent advanced in the West, and our people during the First World War and the National War, for another time, maintained their loyalty and gave their lives for the understanding that the banner must wave so forever.

An ideal in the hands of an ideal man reaches the most elevated values and turns into the charm of victory and accomplishment. If the people who represent such an ideal are not the correct people for the task, then that banner or standard turns into a pennant under which common low whims and ambitions are expressed. Although such a pennant is able to bring together the children in the street, driving them to strike the targets, as if in a game, it is not capable of realizing the emotions and aspirations that reside in the depths of the souls of our people.

A person of ideals is, first of all, a hero of love, who loves God, the Almighty Creator devotedly and feels a deep interest in the whole of creation under the wings of that love, who embraces everything and everybody with compassion, filled with an attachment to the country and people; they care for children as the buds of the future, they advise the young to become people of ideals, giving them high aims and targets, who honors the old with wholehearted regard and esteem, who develops bridges over the abysses to connect and unite the different sections of society, and who exerts all their efforts to polish thoroughly whatever may already exist of harmony between people.

A true person of ideals is also a person of wisdom. While observing everything from the comprehensive realm of reason, they also assess everything with the measures of their appreciative heart, testing them through the criteria of self-criticism and self-supervision, kneading and forming them in the crucible of reason, and always trying to possess and take further the radiance of the mind and the light of the heart in equal harness.

A person of ideals is a true example of responsibility to the society in which they live. To reach their targets, the first of which is, of course, the pleasure of their Creator, they sacrifice everything that God has bestowed on them, without giving the matter a second thought; they have no fear or concern for anything worldly, their heart is captivated by nothing other than God; they have neither ambition for individual happiness nor worry about unhappiness; they are a savior, a hero of the spirit, they do not mind being in hellfire, so long as their ideals and their country are everlastingly firm, stable, and permanent.

A person of ideals and high standing feels respect for the values they are attached to with profound self-supervision, performing their duties in the exhilaration of worship, and living as a hero of love and enthusiasm. Agreeing with and abiding by the truth with minutely meticulous sensitivity they always exercise their preference for sublime ideals. They are always in a struggle in the depths of their heart, a struggle to be the master of their self at all times; they have been sentenced to being a slave to the truth, they are disinterested and indifferent to positions and titles, and they see fame, covetousness, and fondness of comfort and ease as a fatal poison. That is why such people always win where they have an opportunity to win and turn unfavorable circumstances to their advantage.

Walking on this path along with the glorious spirits, such a person is so sincerely devoted to the Will of God that the storms of ambitions which hit them intensify and consolidate their sense of right, justice, and right-mindedness; floods of hatred, grudge, and malice enthuse the springs of love and compassion in their soul; they ignore and tread upon the gifts and blessings that ordinary people are caught up with and they oppose retaliation. If we are to think of such heroes of ideals at their true horizon, a place which perplexes the mind, then we are able to picture a person with an almost prophet-like resoluteness; superhuman pictures flow into our feelings from the doors which have been opened by these associations, and our house of imagination overflows with historical examples of heroism. Thus, are we enthralled by the loyalty and sincerity of Uqba ibn Nafi in the African deserts, enraptured by the bravery and intrepidity of Tariq ibn Ziyad after crossing Gibraltar, lost in admiration of Fatih (Mehmed II) and his resolution, entranced by Gazi Osman Pasha in Plevne, and we salute with reverence the lions of Gallipoli on whose heads bombs and shells were showered and who faced onslaught with a smile on their face.

We do not need anything else but exemplary people of high character and ideals. These exalted souls of the highest ideals will realize the re-establishment of our nation in the coming years. These heroic people, the yeast of whose existence is faith, love, wisdom, and insight, have not yielded to or been shaken by the numerous attacks that came from within and without over almost ten centuries. Perhaps they have shrunk a bit and become a little smaller. However, by acquiring some strength and firmness, they have come to a level where they can settle their accounts with the future, and have observed the age and bided their time to take over the duty with an extraordinary power of spirit.

It is a fact that over the last few ages, love, wisdom, insight, and the consciousness of responsibility have shrunk and simple daily matters have replaced the great ideals. Of course, it is not possible to say that we have done nothing in the name of reform within that period. However, the things put forward remain nothing more than low mimicry and sound effects. Such blind imitation, as a disguise for the introduction of vice and immorality into the thought of the nation, and as a means that leads to the destruction of its spirit, has brought about more harm than good. When the nation was bleeding from the injuries inflicted, one after another, on community's stamina, the real problem was not diagnosed, the way to cure and treat it was not known or defined, and incorrect treatment and meddling caused the masses to be paralyzed. The effects of the crises of the last few ages are still making themselves felt today in flares, eruptions, and centrifugal outbursts of rage.

Therefore, just like before, if we do not deal with the true causes of the problems, if we do not approach and treat individual, familial, and social problems with the ability, sensitivity, and skill of surgeons, if we are not saved from the swamp of vice, immorality, and filthy affairs and dealings from which we have been struggling to extricate ourselves for the last few ages, we will run into errors, one after the other, while looking for remedies; our crises will get much worse and deepen, and we will never be relieved from the vicious circle of crises and depressions.

It doesn't matter if those who hold the reins continue in their age-old obstinacy. We have deep absolute trust in the ideal generations whose thoughts, feelings, and actions turn to the future, who are attached and devoted to their country, people, and ideals, who are focused to serve and contribute to people, indeed to all of humanity, who are taut and ready to be released, like the string of a bow, to serve all with the understanding and consciousness of responsibility. We trust that they will tackle and overcome all negativity and make the newest developments come true. One day, their strong desires and wishes, their love and longing to serve people will penetrate into all sections of society and will turn into seeds that flourish wherever they fall. This approach, which will eradicate the so-called realities of materialism and corporeality, will certainly embroider once more the canvas of its spirit with its own worldview and plan of action.

DETERMINISM IN HISTORY

The perfection and happiness of the generations of tomorrow will be the product of today's generous souls and men of action. It is self-delusion and self-consolation to expect perfect and orderly tomorrows from the wearied, discouraged, slovenly, and vagrant masses who today have given themselves to comfort and lethargy. Tomorrows will develop and flourish in the womb of today; they will be nurtured and nourished by the breasts of today, and thus will reach their prime. As our existence today, with its good and bad sides, carries the traces of yesterday, so too will our tomorrows be copies of today, copies which have developed, expanded, and emerged from individuality and become part of society. Our national life, with its particular colors and qualities, is like a river draining from the plains, mountains, and springs of the past, flowing into the future with its own hues and tones; while advancing toward the future, this river takes up and drives along the characteristics of the places through which it flows. If we look attentively at this river upon which we are also flowing, we will perceive our ancestors' touch, their footprints, excitement, worries, ideals, and the products of their minds and muscles within its flow and currents. Therefore, we can assume that they are our source of life and that we are the sap of future generations with our historical dynamic.

If the gist of such an inheritance can be grasped, the spirit of a nation will always remain young and survive eternally, no matter if the world on all sides gets older, if time changes completely and if ages alter; those who came before will go and those who are gone will be followed by newcomers. Therefore, if in such a change and transformation, Abu Bakr evolves into Umar ibn Abd al-Aziz, if Umar transforms into Fatih, if Ali's spirit becomes that of Battal Ghazi's, and if the Lions of Badr manifest themselves in the depth of the spirit and essence in Manzikert, Kosovo, and Gallipoli, then it means that everything is directed toward eternity. I think the magical formula for renewal and staying forever young must be this. Sacrifices from our individual lives will form the basis for our national existence and continuance. Facing all difficulties with a smile will guarantee eternal life both in this world and the hereafter. The heroic characters who surpass all the heroes in the utopias and who can prepare the future for us and humanity are those who make the best use of the stages of life, from the rose-colored early period when we came to realize ourselves in the colorful and exuberant world of youth, to the period in which maturity is superior, with strength, power, and willpower, to the steady, dignified, self-possessed periods of old age. These heroes are the people who take every step carefully and thoughtfully through these stages; they are those who are ready and willing to sacrifice for others something from their own lives at every bend in the path of life; they are those who, even while dying, die with their faces turned to the higher realms and who are full of love for people, of their own choice and will. Such unknown heroes will always walk and act in this way, of their own free choice and will always run in front, but never put themselves forward for a reward; they will always live from generation to generation as a good recollection or memory, and desire to meet their death in such a way that "it is said a forlorn passed away."

It is impossible for us to promise something for the future of the world and to survive in our tomorrows if we do not raise people with these characteristics, if we do not give them the opportunities to represent these dynamics, or if we do not arrange the different stages of their lives on the networks of such dynamics of the soul and essence of life. If we accept the period we are now in as the basis of the golden slice of the time ahead, such a basis must be appreciated and used well; we must use it with insight, consciousness, comprehension, and patience. This foundation must be made open to the future, yet we still must preserve the spirit and essence; its facets that are open to interpretation should be allowed to acquire a richness that will be able to embrace the future, so that our tomorrows will not develop disconnected from today. If this foundation is neglected, a poor outcome is inevitable. For, considering the spirit of religion and the principles of the natural laws that govern the universe (*shariat al-fitriyya*), wherever the causes are neglected—within the plan of causes, of course—it is completely incorrect to assume that the consequences related to those causes will take place. Determinism (*mu'ayyaniyyat*), which we are always able to observe within natural phenomena is true for historical events as well, conditionally and to a certain degree. The events and persons that have become history now were like seeds which were sown in the soil of history or like eggs that were kept in the incubator of history, and can be considered as the sources of the foundation on which the present is formed and molded. Likewise, the causes that are scattered like seeds on the slopes of the hill of history—again from the perspective of causality—are the factors or causes that will determine the consequences to be shaped by wisdom, colored by justice, expressed in stability, and formalized with integrity.

Indeed, has it not happened thus so far? Are the darkest days that were once lived through not the result of the dirty doings and affairs of previous periods? Did not the Flood gush out of the soil on which the sinners who once defied the Prophet Noah tread? Were the winds blown in *Ahqaf*, that turned its land

upside down, not an action to purify the site that the tribe of *'Ad*
had sullied (Qur'an 46:21)? Was the sacrifice of Sodom and
Gomorrah not the alms given by Earth to the Heavens in recompense for the atrocities committed there? Were the discord,
ignorance, and misinterpretation of the world by the Central
Asian nations, which became wolves waiting at one another's
doors, not the reasons why they were destroyed by Genghis
Khan and Khulagu in ancient history, and why they have suffered in modern times under the ruthless reigns of Communism,
Socialism, and Capitalism? Were not the sighs, groans, and wailings of the oppressed, from the hopeless cries of Carthage to the
innocent, hair-raising cries of the early Christians, cries which
rose to the Heavens, the reasons why the pomp of the Roman
Empire turned to rubble? Was the understanding that some
among them were viewed as "pariahs" not the cause for India
being trodden down by imperial ambitions over such a long
period of time? Even in the recent history, almost all of those
who betrayed that great state of Ottomans and their honorable
nation, a nation which was considered to be the element of balance in the regions from the inlands of Africa to the Balkans, and
thence to some Asian countries, paid many times greater a cost
in return for their betrayal. Was it not the injustice, tyranny, and
persecution of Lenin, Stalin, Hitler, Mussolini, and the like, who
were more evil and greater despots than the most malicious
oppressors in history, that caused not only their views, but also
their statues to be dismantled and thrown away, like malignant
nodes and cysts from the body of humanity?

Despite all the tyranny and unfair treatment they suffered,
the first Muslims drowned their enemies within their own enmity, and with their justice they raised their flags all over the
world. Badr and the conquest of Makka were the domination of
justice and fairness; Uhud was the victory of innocence and
unfair treatment. As their swords were in the hands of their

hearts, their victories followed one upon the other. During that blessed period, what appeared to be fields of defeat turned out to be fields and zones of victory and triumphal arches on the way to the future. In contrast, since the time when might took hold of the sword and since the tongue of the heart has been chained, has not every material domination and rule in the guise of success brought about crushing defeat and complete failure in the spirit, thus turning the zones of victory into arenas where pangs of separation, bitterness of heart, mental pain, longing, and regret patrol?

Until now, no matter under what name, title, or form evil nurtures evil and oppression evolves into a vicious cycle of oppression, all those who have sown sedition have always reaped evil. However, those who sow the seedlings of good always reap good and abundance. Occasionally, although the consequences of good or bad attempts are delayed, their season comes and they will certainly appear, blossom, and make the oppressors groan in pain. As for the oppressed, they become a means of salvation and bliss. Years, or sometimes ages, may pass between cause and effect; but when the preordained time of the effect comes, it makes itself so perceived that the consequence for the innocent, for the guiltless, is Paradise absolutely, and for the disobedient and the oppressor it is hell-fire absolutely.

It is possible to interpret all this in terms of cause and effect in the essence of history; in fact, just as it is possible to interpret this in the sense of justice in the natural laws that govern the universe, so too can it be accepted as an important cause in the cycle of history. There are probably many causes behind historical events, yet the Owner of Infinite Power makes the causes a veil to His acts and makes our world surrounded by them. They are a mysterious blessing, just like the attribute of willpower, which He bestowed upon humanity, and are our material and necessary accessories which we use to fulfill our responsibilities.

In this respect, just as sometimes a little effort can be the initial step of a very important formation, so too a wrong opinion or a mistaken act can bring about several unpleasant results. We can therefore expect happy, colorful tomorrows and blessed ornaments in which all humanity will be interested to emerge from the miniature embroideries worked with the idea of good by some fortunate generations of today.

OUR PHILOSOPHY OF LIFE

S ome live without thinking; some only think, but cannot
put their thoughts into practice. However, we have an
obligation to live thoughtfully and while living, by producing the freshest combinations, to develop more and varied
approaches to thinking. Those who live without thinking are
the objects of the philosophy of others. Such persons always run
from pattern to pattern, ceaselessly changing molds and forms,
hectically struggling their whole life through, in deviations of
thoughts and feelings, in personality disorders, and in metamor-
phoses of character and appearance, never being able to become
their own selves. Although from time to time they share the
achievements of society and benefit here and there from the
occasional breezes of corresponding events, as if those breezes
had some affect on their thought, consciousness, or willpower,
they can never ease nor enliven their spirits with their own,
freely-chosen merits and virtues, nor can they direct them to the
infinite. These people always resemble a pond of water which is
infertile, barren, stagnant, and marred by a bad smell. Far from
being able to express anything that is in the slightest way life-
enhancing, it is inevitable that such people will become like a
life-threatening bundle of viruses or a nest of microbes.

These people are so shallow in their thoughts and so superficial in their views that they imitate everything they hear or see,
like children, drifting along behind the masses, hither and thither, never finding an opportunity to listen to themselves or be
aware of or examine their worth; in fact, they never perceive

that they have values peculiar to themselves. They live their lives as if they were slaves who can never accept freedom from their corporeal and bodily feelings; they evaluate every opportunity they have had and will have within the narrow frames of corporeality; they turn their heart, willpower, feelings, and consciousness, which are the greatest gifts of God to human beings, into a worthless medium of corporeal pleasures, causing people to lead their lives in bohemianism. Such people's passion for rank, title, position, fame, interest, profit, luxury, and living are the most prominent factors determining their acts, deeds, and activities. Consciously or unconsciously, they find themselves caught up in one or more such fatal nets every day and slaughter their souls over and over again in the most wretched of deaths.

Such people, who have neither a past nor a future, say, like Omar Khayyam, "The past and the future are all a tale / Try to enjoy it, do not ruin your life," and follow their animal instincts. They regard the world as a meadow, a pasture on which to graze, in which to live, despite their human emotions and faculties. In fact, they continuously thrash about in a swamp of decadence.

On the other hand, there are those who live thoughtful lives and who, according to their level, turn every hour or day of their lives into a launch for the freshest thoughts and ideas; they lead their lives within the extraordinariness, surprises, and charms of being always beyond time; they drink the past like a blessed spring, breathe it in and fill their lungs with it like a beautiful scent, studying it like an enlightening book, and walk into the future so equipped; they embrace the past with all the warmth of their hearts, color it with their hopes, mold it with their zeal and willpower. As to the present, they accept it as the centre for developing strategies, the workshop for producing the necessary technology, the bridge for crossing over from theory to practice, in order to realize their ideals; thus, they always try to be beyond time and place.

While evaluating the creation and time from this perspective and leaving the narrow confines of material and corporeal life, they go forth into the vastness of the worlds of thinking and wander about the slopes, open to the infinite, of another world which has the dimensions of eternity in this transitory and perishable life. In this way they aim for the infinite with their thoughts, emotions, and aspirations; they observe the richness of being a human in the divine vastness they dig in the depths of their hearts; and with the nets they set up in their hearts, they try to hunt the surprises which no eyes have ever seen, no ears have heard, and which the human imagination cannot conceive or picture. They do all this in such a way that their learning, spiritual knowledge, and acquisitions, which are immeasurable, always show them the lofty realms, even the highest ones, and promise that each of them shall become a heavenly dove. You can call such people, who think and live in this way and who turn their lives into an orchard where abundant trees of thoughts have been planted, men of wisdom or heroes of belief-oriented philosophy. No matter how you define them, it is a fact that since ancient times the enlightened people who have woven history, like delicate and elegant lace, have always been raised from among those high spirits. Brahmanism, Buddhism, Confucianism, Taoism, and Zoroastrianism, which resemble philosophical systems rather than religion, are each a gift to humanity from such heroes of spirituality.

In the murmur of the long currents of thought of the past, you can hear the voiced compositions of such edifices of thought. In the four corners of the world, whether in the ancient or the new world, different worldviews and styles of living, and the cultural richness and universal accumulations of civilizations are always the product of the reflective, meditative harvest of such heroic people. In spite of many alterations and much distortion and the fact that people have been distanced from their essence, we can comfortably say that a great majority of the people in the world still long for that old spirit, essence, and content; yet this is in contradiction with how they live today. Until people take as reference the heroic representatives of the unadulterated, unaltered essence of their own, we will naturally continue to have such a good opinion of others.

While we are trying to renew ourselves and remain connected tightly to our own spiritual roots, what falls on us as a duty today is to raise heroes who know how to urge themselves on from their own souls, that is, who can reinterpret and voice today the music of our yesterdays without being caught or entangled in anything; those who can make us always feel the enthusiasm of our hearts in a different hue every time. In fact, until we raise them, it is obvious that we will continue to be ruined at the hands of strange novices who do not know what to do or how to do it. During this time, the whole of humanity will try to fill the places of the universal and eternal values which their consciences seek, but which they unfortunately can never find within their minds, or within their ancient tales, anecdotes, legends, and myths; thus, they will continually drift toward dissatisfaction and from dissatisfaction to crisis, and from crisis to destruction.

The fact that we did not have a system of thought or philosophy of life which constitutes the spiritual roots of our national culture and which is based on Islamic dynamics means that we have suffered great misery and wretchedness; we have not been alone in this, a large part of the world that is related to us has also suffered so. It is necessary to distinguish our system of thought and philosophy of life from that which is the system of wisdom of Al-Kindi, Al-Farabi (Al-Pharabius), Ibn Rushd (Averroes), and in a sense that of Ibn Sina (Avicenna). They were thinkers who also were the translators of the system of Greek philosophy that is pooled in the thoughts and concepts of

Aristotle, whereas the roots of our system of thought lie in the Heavens, which is as old as eternal past (*azal*), and which is newer than the new, which is able to embrace every age. It is derived from and based on Divinity (*lahut*), divine Might and Majesty (*jabarut*), God's supreme dominion (*malakut*), and human nature (*nasut*); its origins are definite and known, that is luminous and which is based on and related to the truth of being created. If such an interpretation is comprehended within its own spirit and essence, it will be possible even at the present time to put forward and realize our own system of thought, which consequently will bring about serious renewals worldwide, opening up much richer ways and routes for all.

Since the middle of the fifteenth century, there have been many attempts initiated toward developing this idealized system of thought. However, they have never been able to reach the desired objectives. Although this observation is open to contention in certain respects, in general it is true. From Hodjazade to Zeyrek, from Mustafa Reşit Pasha to the architects of Constitutional monarchy,[32] from these to the latest workers of thought, many, whether sincere or not, have tried to find answers to this search and expectations in the collective conscience. However, some became entangled in the *Tahafuts*[33] of Ibn Rushd and Imam Ghazali, some drowned and perished in the whirlpools of the French Revolution and Auguste Comte, while some were kept busy in the delirium and obsession of Durkheim. They were always active, but they have never taken into account the age in which they lived, and have either gone beyond fantasy or routed thousand-year-old national values into bewilderment by treating their whims and fancies as their god. I wish we could have overcome such vexations and negativities by now. How I wish we could overcome such contrariness and develop a system of thought and a national philosophy nurtured by our own sources!

Let me express this concisely; because the angles of feeling, perception, and interpretation of the natural phenomena are different, if we do not have a strong foundation of thought or a system of philosophy on which to build everything, our views will always be in contradiction and we will devour one another in a web of opposition and conflict. Tomorrow, as well as today, can be our property only by means of this strong method and system, and by means of a common manner or style, which all the generations will voluntarily share. If we do not have such unity in our thoughts, feelings, and manner of life, it will remain nothing but grandiose wishful thinking to talk about national unity and solidarity, both today and tomorrow. For in every system, national logic, thinking, reasoning, and the spiritual inspirations (*waridat*) are very important. To the extent that a system of thought arises from a nation's own mind, conscience, and world of emotions, can the unity of feelings, logic, and reasoning, and the ease of living together as a nation be realized. On the other hand, where a nation's feelings, thoughts, interpretations, and styles clash with one another, and where reasoning and rationality are in contradiction, actions and activities would yield no fruit, even though there are a great many of them taking place. In such cases, complete devastation is also likely to happen. In a society where such conflict and commotion of understanding and interpretation are experienced, every effort will continually clash and break with another, just like the waves of the sea, and by pouring into its own pool of inertia everything will keep on whirling in a vicious circle. There is some seen and unseen wisdom in the clash of the waves at sea, their breaking and their calming of one another. However, there is only stagnation, rot, disintegration, and self-annihilation in similar collisions and clashes if found within a society. In such a society, everyone seems to be a wolf at the other's door and every thought a project of death; and even if heavenly blessings shower continuously on that society, it will be like clothes under attack from moths; even historical values are subject to attack and becoming moth-eaten, the sacred is face to face with the danger of destruction; and they don't recieve loyalty from the old, nor chivalry from the young; the young people, whom we expect to become heroes, to be the dynamic power that will carry the standard of the bright future on their shoulders, instead swear at the flag and curse the history of their country, considering the future as the arena in which they will perform all their impetuousness and insanity. The old and the intelligentsia, who indulge in hair-raising heedless-ness, act almost as the advocates of such decadence; in their expressions, writings, and TV shows they incite bohemianism in the spirit and devastate the understanding and discernment of people, as if they were pouring acid on them.

During such a period, the seats of science and knowledge are not able to evoke a love and thought of knowledge. Those who represent power and authority become the pawns of par-ticular ideologies and devour one another; logic, reasoning, and inspiration are condemned to walk in the narrow aisles of enig-matic signs and expressions. In a society in which such contrari-ness and vexations develop, idleness, ambition and vanity replace thinking, life becomes nothing but a torture.

Our system of thought or philosophy of life, however, is related to not only the world of existence, but also to the realm of pre-existence, and to whatever is beyond existence. It also deals with all natural phenomena and things which lie beyond as a whole; it is vast enough to define the manner of our entire lives in continuity. It is with such a system that society, in its smallest particle, the individual, is able to realize the universal justice awaited on Earth and respond to all the expectations of humanity by stimulating individuals to act morally; in this way, society is fed with spirit, morality, virtue, and contemplation and thus reaches a state of being renewed as itself. Thus, our understanding of civilization and cultural richness becomes a desirable good, demanded, and sought after all over the world; we are therefore able to extend our helping hands to the rest of the world to present comfortably our ideals of humanity, our philosophy of morality, our understanding of virtue, and our acceptance and interpretation of justice. Again, as a result of having acquired such a level and position, like all the power sources of a state, administrative dynamics and social and economic principles will spring out from the people's own spirit and in this way society will save itself from all sorts of "dependence." So far, the tacit dependence which we have been carrying like a yoke around our necks due to our weaknesses and indebtedness, has paralyzed and caused inertia in our political, economic, and judicial systems, just as it did in our administrative system. In the past, our golden generations, who had once made Anatolia one of the most cultivated, prosperous countries of the world, developed and established their own administrative, political, and judicial systems out of the materials of their own spirit. They did not let any thinking, system, or understanding enter the institutions of the people, which were safeguarded like their homes, family pride, and good name, without having checked it by their own criteria and measures. Far from letting these in, even after they had struggled with nearly the entire world and experienced a temporary defeat, and even while they were retreating wounded and shaken, but ever hopeful, with faith, and with great zeal and desire, they tried to preserve their own origins, gathered around the consciousness of history, and held tightly to the dynamics to which they owe their existence— as expressed in a hadith, they "held (them) tightly between their teeth and their palate." Their heads were not bent down, but held high, their understanding, acceptance, and interpretation of the world and the Hereafter were sound and intact, and they advanced toward a fresh revival without pausing for a breath.

Today, when dawns follow new dawns, from the perspective of our own horizon of wisdom, if we are able to evaluate soundly and once more make use of the world in which we are now living, if we are able to interpret things and events well, if we are able to determine the basic materials of the inner structure of our own people, and if we are able to attach ourselves to the ideals that exist until eternity, we will always be like our glorious ancestors; we may even advance ahead of them. Indeed, why should the insightful generations not be in advance of those of the past; indeed of all generations? They will take the past, the present, and the future, putting them into perspective all at the same time, evaluating and making the best of them; they will take the traditions, culture, and historical dynamics of the society in which they live under their protection; they will interpret well the cycle of the recurrence of history in the direction of their own renewal.

It is important to recall, once again, that the first responsibility that falls to us is to make felt in the consciences of the generations the effects of pain, suffering, hardship, beliefs adopted and the cultures rooted in direct proportion to their weightiness. This will be done by developing in people the consciousness of history. If we can do this, after a few generations no one living in our land will think of looking for or finding any foreign source for our various institutions beyond our spiritual dynamics.

We will be bringing all the elements of our life tomorrow from the past. If we are able to blend them with the light of our religion and the rays of science and knowledge in the crucible of our culture, we will have prepared the glue of our eternity.

THE GENERATIONS OF HOPE - I

The generations of hope, which are, with respect to the present, the representatives of science, knowledge, faith, morality, and art, are also the architects of the spirits of the people who will succeed us. They will pour out to the needy hearts the purest inspirations of their hearts, which are nourished in the higher realms and they will bring forth the newest formations in all sections of society. The inauspiciousness and waste, the insanity, obsessions, and delirium of successive generations in our near past occurred, to a great extent, because they had not met such a generation of hope.

Within the last few centuries in our history, we have experienced total failure after failure, even in places where we should have succeeded, and have lost mostly in the arenas where we should have won and been victorious. At this time, we treated one another like wolves, and left an inheritance of grudge, hatred, and political greed and ambition to those who came after us; those who were in politics and those who supported them considered every means and action as legitimate and permissible if it were to gain them position for their own team or party; they devised and entered into complex intrigues and deluded themselves that by overthrowing the dominant group and changing the party in power they would change everything and the country would be saved. Neither those in power nor those in the opposition ever understood that it was only possible to reach their stated targets through a performance of revolutionary-like actions directed by thought, knowledge, faith, morality, and virtue. That is why they saw the desired "change" and "transformation" in empty, formal, and meaningless alterations on the exterior only, and in what might have been a huge historical restoration and reformation they became entangled in paints, colors, whitewash, and mere cosmetic changes. Moreover, some, being alienated from our true national values, sold out the ideal of patriotism to Satan in exchange for insignificant things, just like the naïve Faust; and according to the requirements of time and conditions, and some passing interests and gains, they subjected themselves to the madness of being one type of nation on one day and another on another day, yet in fact not being so, but only appearing as if so. They either breathed Turanism once, or mumbled the farmer-peasant nation once, or talked about aristocracy somewhat pretentiously once, or attempted to say democracy once, or winked at communism once, but they never saved themselves from drifting here or there. Particularly with the mixed appetite of our intelligentsia, an appetite that has no scale or criteria, a fancy and fantasy of France at one time, a liking and admiration of England at another, a passion for Germany next, then a love and zeal for America, or some other such country, became the drive behind our interpretation of life and the ports from which we were to sail forth into the future.

In contrast to this, the sense of nationality and religion, which is the common ideal of our people, should be based on a foundation. The foundation should be above all sorts of fantasies, it should exceed the truth of individual spirits, and it should be of a strong faith, of established thought, of sound morality and of virtue that is acknowledged and owned by all souls. It should be stronger than the strongest of all foundations. This is a moral movement, which each and every day leads in the same direction, which is on the course of its own richness of spirituality and understanding of reality, which is open to all kinds of change and new attempts, which revolves around God's pleasure, which is completely immune to considerations of interest and profit, and which will promise the desired salvation to the future generations. Otherwise, while our intellectual world goes down such a twisted path, while our hearts hold a faith that has not yet acquired certainty (*yaqin*), and while they are in utter confusion and disorder, while our minds see so many diverse methods and concepts that have multiple views of civilization, it seems impossible for us to claim the ownership of a spirit and essence—the real property of our nation—to take it under our protection, and to pass it safely to the future generations like a trustworthy keeper.

Many have witnessed and know quite well our near past, the critical periods in which we lost the values that belonged to us. We thought a great deal of producing a new style and philosophy of life for ourselves by combining so many diverse understandings and interpretations, so distant from one another, and so many thoughts that contradict one another. Alas! We have wasted so many lives and are still consoling ourselves with the delusion that we are producing something. As we have not been able to do this so far, it would be impossible for us to do it from now on if we carry on in the same way. For without embracing the roots of spirituality and meaning of our own lives, it will not be possible to reach a new synthesis in thought and a fresh style in expressing ourselves. During this period, far from reaching a new synthesis and style, we have experienced a continuous nausea because of the split in our understanding and feelings and the effects of fluctuating contradictions in our soul. Of course, all the opportunities we received from time to time and the potential strengths and powers we had were completely wasted, lost, and came to naught.

Although it may have seemed that we accomplished some things in the last few centuries, we have not been able to present convincing or admirable work in terms of our own faith, our way of thinking, morality, culture, art, economics, or in our way of administration. Even though there have been some achievements in this period, they proved to be nothing more than "fantasy" or "superficial" things initiated to arouse the desires of youth. These achievements went no further than a couple of dozen insignificant wishes and desires when compared to our real needs, such as the interpretation of the age, an evaluation and appreciation of knowledge and science, a comprehension of the spirit of concord and alliance (*wifaq* and *ittifaq*), and resolving and overcoming the needs and wants which have bent us double for a long time. Our salvation from such narrow views and meager thoughts which enslave our senses and hold us prisoner can only be realized by the heroes of understanding, insight, and God-consciousness, who are conscious of and realize the age we live in, who are lovers of the truth, who are inspired by a longing for knowledge, who are bent under the burden of the true difficulties and troubles of today and of those anticipated in the future, whose acts are the reflection of their inner life and words, whose promises are the breaths of their heart, of people who are able to see beyond the horizon, who feel pain in the actual undesired state and dim future of people, who suffer in order to lift and raise generations to higher levels and shed tears for them like Job, who share the present and future pains and distress of the generation, and who appreciate their happiness and pleasures as the work and gifts of God, becoming ever more thankful for these and being elevated with that thankfulness. These heroes of God-consciousness will take their strength and inspiration from our life and centuries of colorful history, they will breathe into us the spirit of being a nation true and purer than the purest, they will thus enthuse our youth with faith, hope, and ideals of action, and will produce new canals and watercourses in the pool of our national ideals which has been stagnant and inactive in the fatal dam of a long and terrible extinction.

And then we, as the nation, will run to the place of worship where we lost in our hearts through such canals and courses, will shed tears of reunion; by returning to our homes which are as warm as the corners of Paradise, we will meet the reflections of the Paradise we lost long ago; by rediscovering our own schools whose pillars are the search for truth and the love of knowledge, we will meet and be re-introduced to creation through the outlets of schools which are open to the universe; by loving all human beings we will learn how to share everything; by living through more agitation for others we will embrace everybody on the diamond hills of our hearts; by observing and looking into the creation we will be enthused by the sense of art, and in our relations with people we will think with deep inner concerns and sighs, drenched in tears and wrenched by palpitations, and thus express ourselves.

THE GENERATIONS OF HOPE - II

For us to experience a new nationwide resurrection is dependent on a few dozen heroes who will be the life in our bodies and the blood in our veins. A few dozen heroes who will have reached the lights of the truth beyond the horizon of knowledge, who will have controlled and disciplined the demands and desires of their body, paring these down to only the bare necessities. These heroes will always feel in their conscience that they are called to God in a transcendent harmony. They will always communicate His message, sobbing with enthusiasm, speaking with formless words and voices; they will breathe in and out with Him.

As these heroes have dedicated themselves in a willing slavery to truth from the very onset, they will never be servants or slaves to the disorderly wishes, work, and dealings of society. They are conscious of servitude to God in humility and continually act with the observation and understanding of eternity in all their acts. They will lead their life under the shower of inspirations from God. By turning to and forcing the gates of other divine gifts with every inspiration, they will feel their difference for they are blessed with turning one into thousands, and will taste at every incident of extinction, the delights, enjoyments, and pleasures of eternity.

The adventures of the lives of these heroes will be renewed within the frame of faith, knowledge, affection, love, and spiritual pleasures; their horizon of thinking will soar over the vastness which separates the mortal from the eternal. Their capital is knowledge and faith, their base the Owner of the Infinite Might, and their path the way of all the righteous servants of the Truth who have ever lived. They go forward, relying on the invincible power of religion and the surprise favors of God in the guidance of the Prophet to eternity, and so a period of apostasy, unbelief, and atheism will drown and perish in bottomless pits of unnaturalness.

Just as humanity has never lived without faith or knowledge in any period of history, so too have civilizations never been without places of worship or God. Although, by darkening their own horizon with their own hands, humanity has occasionally fallen down into the pits of faithlessness and ignorance, they have stood up with a more consistent, meaningful, speedy, dignified return from every fall, feeling their bond with the Creator more profoundly in their consciences. That is why staying and living in a vacuum of civilization, in relation to places of worship and God, and of humanity, in relation to faith and knowledge, has always been a temporary state, and will continue to be so from now on; until Doomsday and the destruction of the worlds, the thought of the places of worship and God will not be eradicated from the hearts of humanity; human beings will never be completely torn away from their Creator. Consciences are fundamentally open to God; therefore, the temporary darkening of their horizon from time to time will be like an eclipse. The light will follow the darkness, and dawn will follow the sunset; and when it is due, time and whatever is bound with it will launch into the course and orbit that are pre-destined by the irresistible pre-ordained decrees of God in eternity.

All around the world the generations of today are seeking their own essence, the life in their conscience, and the Paradise they once lost. This inclination, even to this degree, will be enough for them to find their hero and reach the line of the Truth. Once their consciences are on the course of their nature and disposition, God is perceived in everything that comes to them through their inner senses.

Moreover, atheism, which rips things from the spirit and the essence they contain and uses them for the sake of its own wishes, ambitions, and fantasies, has started to be beaten down by its own inconsistencies and even to disintegrate. During this time, the spirits that are seeking their own truth have moved into the phase of discovering their own essence. Of course, in this way people will lose their interest in the ordinary things. They will sense their inability, weakness, and helplessness as a point of reference in their hearts, and perceive the point of support and reliance (*nokta al-istinad*) and the point of help and assistance (*nokta al-istimdad*) in the depths of their consciences. Thus, their natures will exhibit extraordinariness, their willpower will rescue them from their narrowness and so they will turn to the will and commands of God, the Infinite, the Eternal.

Again in this process, faith and resoluteness, which are the greatest spiritual dynamic of success, will make everyone achieve the power of their spirit pertaining to the secrets of the divine. This power will enthuse their hope and willpower, will eliminate their disorderliness and inconsistencies, will help them cross the bridges which lead them to being themselves, and will thus enable them to reach God.

The quickest, shortest, safest, and most accurate way for human beings to reach the truth is the way of faith, which is equipped with spiritual and scientific knowledge. The soul has always achieved its most mind-boggling accomplishments and victories in this way. In a place where faith is not fed with knowledge, coercion replaces the truth and law, and one inevitably meets brute force and bullying there. Under such conditions, weapons are often resorted to, money talks, only quick-wit makes its voice heard, and hypocrisy becomes the most desirable and sought-after quality. It is impossible to reach the spirit or essence of the Creation or to observe what lies behind it in such an atmosphere.

On the other hand, our truth is tightly related to the spirit of the infinite. To sense this relationship and to perceive what this relationship promises, we, as a whole nation, have to sacrifice much. It is not possible to talk about such a relationship or connection unless we sacrifice from our individual pleasures and happiness worldly amenities and possibilities, ranks, positions and titles, and even our feelings and ambitions for spiritual prosperity. If this relation and connection are realized, tomorrow's world will be a bright, luminous world in which God is held the Most High, in which the truth will be made a crown and duly respected, and in which interest in power and self-seeking will be seen as a shame, a disgrace.

We feel that we have been on the way to such a luminous world for years. We deal neither with searching for the signs and symptoms of the awaited dawn nor with investigating magical numbers and dates for mysterious future happenings. By evaluating everything that the needle of the compass of our souls shows under the guidance and leadership of Divine realities, we will try to relate and connect ourselves to the Divine Will by means of our own willpower; we will become like those heroic people who spent everything they had on this way; we will use, spend, and sacrifice from our own lives and wealth; we will keep on walking on this way until we meet the Divine Will and what it presents and promises.

Each and every person who has a sense of serious individual responsibility will say, "I have to do this myself. If I do not do it now, to whatever extent I can, then probably no one will do it," and they will run forward to be the first to do it, to bear the flag high. They will do this without competition, without jealousy or envy, without hindering and troubling others, but rather by providing opportunities around them for others to progress. During the dark period we have experienced, some of the things we did knowingly or unknowingly have tarnished our hearts and ruined our spirits; a great majority of our people were not able to pull themselves up or shake themselves off, and thus were unable to awaken to the lights of truth in their essence. They did not reach or acquire the spiritual dynamics that express vitality, which are like water, air and the power for vegetative growth necessary for our revival and resurrection. At least nowadays, instead of searching like an ivy for something apart from ourselves on which we can cling to remain upright and survive, by bringing out our potential power with all its relationships and ties with the beyond and the higher realms, by relying on Him, we continue walking toward Him.

To reach such a standpoint where we can see all, hear all, hold and take away all, and evaluate with a reasoning that is open to inspiration is dependent on revising and renewing this potential power and connection. In short, you never seek the spirit and essence which carries you to existence outside of yourself. Bend your head and listen to your conscience and, by using your essence, your entity like a magnifying glass you will start to travel in the direction of existence from your own essence.

REUNION WITH OURSELVES

The twentieth century was a century of incessant problems and the present continues to be the same. One of those problems is so very deep that it makes us forget all others; it is chronic and resistant to intervention and treatment, and is so urgent that it must not be neglected. This serious problem is the neglect of our values by our own people, especially the young. If it cannot be fully resolved by skilful hands, with no further loss of time, we will find ourselves immersed in a great many undesired ills and misfortunes, and so experience complete failure despite convenient circumstances while new events will appear at the most unexpected times to darken our destiny.

The cancers of negligence, ignorance, indifference, inadequacy, and the fantasy of estrangement and alienation in the entire community appeared in the form of nodules yesterday, and have metastasized within a very short time, spreading rapidly throughout our body, making us fall to our knees. This has happened to such an extent that a distinct "decline" has occurred in each and every circle of society and the color in our people has been washed away. Alas! How many times have we been shaken by such ailments! How many times have we suffered the misfortune of failing and being defeated! How many times have we deteriorated, seeing the dark fate we are doomed with! How many times have we attempted to express our anger at such events! How many times have we felt the inadequacy of being unable to find words against these events, whether they be foul and unbecoming words, or an appropriate response! How many times have we suppressed and quenched our exasperation and palpitations by taking refuge in God! Some of us have been writhing in the currents of such murderous feelings, while others have succeeded only in blaming those who fell into foulness.

However, instead of blaming and calumniating such people, as well as others, for the path they have followed, we should have embraced them with a promise of a new and fresh life; by greeting their enthusiasm and excitement with respect, while finding reasonable causes and excuses for their obsessions and delirium, we should have tried to remove the atmosphere of anger, violence, and terror; by giving them some rights, we should have prepared the ground to discuss matters which were common or mutual between us. It is a fact that our society is one which shelters various thoughts, concepts, and philosophies. Therefore, while advancing on our national course, we came across the French tracks and were influenced, and then were entangled in the German approaches and interpretations. Some time later, we indulged in the English way of thinking, and recently we have been intoxicated with the free American philosophy. Thus we have always placed barriers in our way. It is true that all these concepts, interpretations, and philosophies have negatively affected our national culture. Yet it is also true that such variety and colorfulness can always be appreciated as richness. To me, what is important is that our nation preserves its own values and that the nation revolves in its own orbit. However, having been unable to evaluate such different cultures, each of which is considered to be the latest synthesis by those who support it, we have been caught up and obstructed by trifles, like soil and pebbles encountered while excavating a mine. Like inexperienced miners searching for a mineral seam, they either dig into the soil and rock and assume the shaft leads to rock only, leaving off without seeing the wealth—or they fail to be interested in the mineral seam because they assume that the mine they have entered is merely rock. We have so far had access to many sources of light, but instead of evaluating and making the best use of them for our illumination, we have produced flames and fire from them, allowing the fires to devour us instead of illuminating us.

It is strange that some among us, no matter how little they know, always take others lightly; all who think, even a little, consider themselves to be a philosopher. Those who represent power treat reason and logic as superfluous, but continue on their way in being the executers of brute force. Those in politics make partisanship the ultimate target and sacrifice everything for it on the understanding that they cannot exist without it. Our socio-cultural, political, and economic activities have never been able to emerge from the vicious cycle of opposition and conflict in the web of jealousy, envy, competition, and intolerance. Those who do not even have the maturity of teenagers have used their featherweight toys and olive branches to strike each others' heads; the young, instead of repairing our shaken credit and broken pride, have used the dynamism of their spirits against their own nation and people, causing fissures and gashes in the spirit of the nation.

Why is this so, I wonder! Why do we not love one another while we can? Why do we not establish lasting understandings and friendships? Why can we not share anxiety, grief, afflictions and joy, success, and happiness? I wonder if the effort and struggle on the way to gain hearts is more difficult for us than the effort and struggle of the battlefield. Is the heart of humanity closed to love, tolerance, acceptance of others; does it shy from embracing, and sharing; is it inclined to hatred, malice, coarseness, intolerance, restrictions, and selfishness? I cannot believe that this is true! I swear by God, who creates hearts, that what is richest and deepest cannot be so closed to virtues, yet so open to vice!

The greatest conquerors in the world started with the conquest of the hearts. Their first stop was the hearts of the people and, using those hearts as their base and port, they sailed forth unto other parts of the world. If they had not first entered the hearts of the Anatolian people, they would not have won at Manzikert, the battle between the Seljuk State and the Byzantines in 1071, a battle which opened the gates of Anatolia to the Muslims. The ramparts of Constantinople would not have yielded to attack if it had not felt the promises of the soldiers' hearts beating with sincerity. The web of love and compassion, which emerged first as emotion and interest and later took all hearts and people under its control, welcomed and tolerated those who ran to it of their own choice and free-will, making them listen to legends of love and affection.

So now, if it is not in our history, where did this hatred, malice, enmity, and intolerance come from and how did it infiltrate into our people? While we have felt a deep admiration for France, Germany, England, and more recently America and Japan over the last few eras, why do we hate and undermine one another and live like wolves, devouring one another? Why do we spoil and make life a hell for others? Do we have a personality disorder? And we say, "Yes, and we might as well take refuge in foreign souls," and thus throw our thousand-year-old values into the garbage for the sake of a fantasy.

While we have been making chaos out of nothing for ourselves, so many generations without any base, support, course, targets, ideals, or of course, spiritual knowledge have been raised as the children of whims, ambitions, fancies, and fantastic day-dreams. Such generations, who have lost all metaphysical considerations, are unaware of their national identity, and continue to live deluded in the belief that they have found the answer to the question "who am I?" in the out-moded disposable philosophies that they have scrounged from the seven continents. They have struggled in the net of the ebb and flow of the material, they have lived tongue-tied and heartless, and from time to time confused religion with epic tales and historic legends; they have sacrificed morality with the arrival of permissiveness, tainted the understanding of art with the hues of lust, turned poetry and music into shamelessness, and finally found themselves right in the middle of a killing arena in which countless contradictions and conflicts ruthlessly war against each other. Indeed, the consequences cannot be thought otherwise.

And then these generations attacked everything with wrath and fury; they denigrated and despised our past; they lost their trust and their own trustworthiness along with their faith; and they felt the loss and absence of affection deeply, as well as that of humane feelings. Moreover, during this period, they were surrendered to the hands of foreign consciences; their upbringing and education were left to foreigners; they were raised like babies in the nurseries of foreign countries, becoming closer to foreigners than to us; they were the victims of different ideologies, shivering because of the distance and coldness between them, though they were in fact close enough to feel each other's body heat. It is these people whose faith was pierced with thousands of doubts and uncertainties, whose trust was shaken from its foundations, whose hopes were routed in confusion, whose hearts were like the bed of a river long dried up, whose human feelings were entrusted to hatred, malice, and enmity, whose hearts become the orbit for and hunting ground of so many fears, who were always delivered to the tides of purposelessness and aimlessness, and therefore beaten by the distances, whose horizons were plunged in darkness, with no hope of light, who, even when ascending, were in decline, and who became false, artificial, and temporary, as if their essence had been squeezed out and they remained standing, with only a husk.

In fact it is very difficult to breathe life into such a walking corpse, for it is alienated from this life of ours and reacts against its own values. On the other hand, despite everything, it falls to us again to support and raise it. Our belief is that when the Divine Will flows into our willpower like life that this corpse will rise as if having heard the trumpet of Israfil[34] and cry out once more its good fortune, prosperity, and felicity. In fact, it will not be easy to fill the emptiness and repair the damage that was produced in the body of society by the great negligence of the last few eras. However, the heirs of thought in the world, who have so many times transformed not only their own misfortune, adversity, and disgrace, but also that of all those who were oppressed, wronged, and unjustly treated, will certainly overcome such a terrifying misfortune, and establish a peaceful and prosperous Paradise for others while continuing to inhabit their world of bare necessities. They will naturally fill the voids in society with the expanse of their tolerance and leniency; this is their responsibility. They will ignore the faults of others looking at them through the binoculars of their own faults which are, perhaps, the cause of the faults of others. Without pressuring, ill-treating, or making others suffer under the guilt of their faults, such heirs will demonstrate a number of alternatives for ridding oneself of these faults, alternatives for rehabilitation and improvement.

We are aware that it is not possible to change everything overnight; we do not await a miracle. In a society whose values have been so long overturned, and which has been accustomed to such discord, it will of course take more than a little effort to replace atheism with faith, arbitrariness with discipline, chaos with order, immorality with morality, lust with love for God, and personal interests and gains with altruism. We are sure that the eradication of atheism, which long ago sat itself on the throne of faith, of this too free and easy behavior which has toppled moral values, of the depravity and unfruitfulness which profits from the lack of discipline, is not, and will never be easy. It is not easy to replace all these and establish in their place what God wills and what the Prophet advises. For all the criteria which make masses into a society and which make a society into a true society, were routed by deviant ideologies, nihilistic thoughts, and defiant deliriums all over the world. At the same time, a sense of responsibility was eradicated from our hearts, and the vigorous youth drank their fill of bohemianism; everyday a new fantasy pulled the masses along behind it; and certain free, independent spirits, and intoxicated natures expressed their defiance, rejection, and contempt of all our values, allowing themselves to be swept away in the currents whose destination and destiny are always uncertain.

Now it falls to us, to everybody who loves this country and this people, to eliminate all this disorderliness and to reawaken our stagnant activity in accordance with the horizon of own philosophy. By drawing on the innermost part of the national spirit and by using our willpower as much as we can, and with a resoluteness sharpened by so many years of oppression, wrongs, and ill-treatment, just like the apostles of Jesus and the first Muslims, we should say, "Let's get on with it," and try to go everywhere in the understanding that "where there is a person, so there should be faith, consideration for others, and knowledge"; and thus we should make our lives gain the depth of moving from one emigration to another. From this time on, we should try to weave the lace of our lives on the canvas of thought and action of the heroes of truth who have won the pleasure of God.

We believe that almost everyone on Earth will appreciate and admire hands extended to them by hearts of such caliber. If they succeed, the possessors of such mature, sound, and dignified willpower will be the standard-bearers of our religion, country, language, and ideals; they will travel all over the world, will be met like Khidr wherever they go, and what they present to people will be accepted and drunk like the elixir of life. Wherever they visit, they will set forth into the infinite in a friendship like that of Moses and Khidr, will build protective ramparts and defensive walls for those who await Dhu al-Qarnayn[35] and will point out the roads that lead to the resurrection to those recluses who have been spending their lives in caves for years. Who knows, they will perhaps take first glimmers of the thought of the greatest, the most comprehensive Renaissance wherever they go; this has been awaited for centuries.

NOTES

[1] See Bukhari, *Janaiz*, 79.

[2] A'raf 7: 28; Hud 11: 49.

[3] See Ra'd 13:11, Anfal 8:53.

[4] *i'la al-kalimatullah*: Knowing the highness and value of God's word and Islamic truths, spreading His name and word and teaching them to others.

[5] Hurufis: The sect, of the past, which drew conclusions of letters, used onomancy.

[6] Qurtubi, *al-Jami'u Li-ahkam-il Qur'an*, 4/251.

[7] Some younger Companions who had not had a chance to attend the Battle of Badr wanted to fight on the battlefield. Blinded by their willingness, they could not appreciate the Prophet's wise judgment to resist the enemy by defending the city, Madina. This is considered to be *zalla*, a lapse.

[8] Qurtubi, *al-Jami'u Li-ahkam-il Qur'an*, 4/251.

[9] *al-Jami'u Li-ahkam-il Qur'an*.

[10] Abu Dawud, *Adab*, 114; Tirmidhi, *Zuhd*, 39; *Adab*, 57; Ibn-i Maja, *Adab*, 37.

[11] Qurtubi, *al-Jami'u Li-ahkam-il Qur'an*, 16/36.

[12] Tirmidhi, *Fitan*, 7.

[13] Ibn Maja, *Fitan*, 8.

[14] *Musnad*, 6/396.

[15] See note 7.

[16] This council is called *ahl al hal wal 'aqd*, meaning "those who can bring issues to a solution."

[17] The Muhajirun are the early Muslims who emigrated to Madina from Makka and the Ansar are the locals of Madina who helped those emigrants and the early Muslims.

[18] *Miraj*: Prophet Muhammad's ascension, or night journey, to the Heavens.

[19] *Kawthar*: Paradisiacal water, beverage; abundance.

[20] *Sakina*: peace, serenity, calmness, tranquillity. The angels and spiritual beings through whom such a state descends are also called so.

[21] Babiali Raid (1913): The armed raid carried out by the Ittihad ve Terakki Party on the Central Office of the imperial Ottoman government in order to take over the administration.

[22] Khidr, peace be upon him, is a blessed person whose name is mentioned in the Qur'anic commentaries and the hadith (Bukhari, *Tafseer*, 249). Khidr (or Khadir) literally means green or a place with abundant green plantation. According to a hadith Khidr was named so because he sat over a barren white land and it turned green with

plantation after (his sitting over it) (Bukhari, *Anbiya*, 29). It is also reported that since Khidr drank from a fountain in Paradise, every place he stepped on turned green (Makdisi, III, 78).

23 One of the prophets whose name is mentioned in the Qur'an (37:123-130), Elijah (or Elias), peace be upon him, lived in the ninth century BC and came to revive the faith and law of Moses among the people of Israel. It is reported that he was raised to a different level of life and he meets with Khidr every pilgrimage season (see Nursi, *The Letters*, The First Letter).

24 Judi: The mountain where the Ark of Prophet Noah was landed according to the Qur'an, Hud 11:44: *Then the word went forth: "O earth! Swallow up your water, and O sky! Withhold (your rain)!" and the water abated, and the matter was ended. The Ark rested on (Mount) Judi, and the word went forth: "Away with those who do wrong!"* Mount Judi is located in south-east Turkey very close to Turkish-Iraqi border. With many caves, easy slopes, and certainly its hand-palm shaped top, its landscape looks suitable to accommodate after the flood. It is also reported that Judi might be the name of a mountain range across Mosul, Jizra, and Damascus.

25 *Ghassal*: The person who conducts the ritual bath for the dead in Islam.

26 *Tuba al-Jannah*: Name of a tree in Paradise, with flowers and ripe fruit of every imaginable—and unimaginable kind.

27 *Ihsan*: a. favor, benevolence, kindness; b. a restraining, keeping clear from sin or impropriety; c. acting and praying as if seeing God, and being conscious of that He sees you though you do not see Him.

28 *A'raf*: The plain, field, which is in between, or separating, the Paradise and the Hell

29 A Turkish proverb, each and every one is responsible for himself or what he has done; what I do is none of your business, you will not be questioned or accounted for what I do, so mind your own business.

30 He who succeeds is acknowledged as an able person; I managed something now, I am able, I have the potentiality, or full control, therefore I will try to make the best of the opportunities arisen and harvest what it yields; if you are able then you too do it, if don't leave me alone.

31 National War: Turkish war to save Turkey from invasion by the Allies after the First World War (1999-1922).

32 The new constitution and parliamentarian system in the Ottoman history, which was announced first in 1876 but did not properly operate due to unending warfare until a second announcement in 1908.

33 *Tahfut at Tahafut* (Incoherence of the Incoherence) by Ibn Rushd and *Tahafut al-Falasifa* (Incoherence of Philosophers) by Imam Ghazali are two famous works in the history of philosophy.

34 The archangel who will sound *Sur*, the trumpet at the Day of Resurrection.

35 Dhu al-Qarnain: "He of the two horns." His name is mentioned in the eighteenth chapter of the Qur'an. Various sources report him as a messenger or a prophet, where as 'Ali, the fourth Caliph, says he was a righteous servant of God, neither a prophet nor a king.

INDEX